R. Gupta's®

MANIPUR GK HANDBOOK

With

MULTIPLE CHOICE QUESTIONS

2020
REVISED EDITION

Ramesh Publishing House, New Delhi

Published by
O.P. Gupta *for* Ramesh Publishing House

Admin. Office
12-H, New Daryaganj Road, Opp. Officers' Mess,
New Delhi-110002 ✆ 23261567, 23275224, 23275124

E-mail: info@rameshpublishinghouse.com
Website: www.rameshpublishinghouse.com

Showroom
- Balaji Market, Nai Sarak, Delhi-6 ✆ 23253720, 23282525
- 4457, Nai Sarak, Delhi-6, ✆ 23918938

Book Code: R-954

ISBN: 978-93-5012-703-2

HSN Code: 49011010

WHO'S WHO

N. Biren Singh

Governor : Dr. Najma A. Heptulla

Chief Minister : N. Biren Singh

MINISTERS

Sl.No.	*Name*	*Portfolio(s)*
1.	**N. Biren Singh**	C.M., Home, Finance, Power, Public Works, Transport, Personnel, Planning, Minor Irrigation, Minority & OBC, General Administration, Sericulture, Tourism, IT, vigilance and other departments not specifically allocated to any other ministers.
2.	**Y. Joykumar Singh**	Deputy CM., Excise, Taxation, Science and Technology, Economics and Statistics and Civil Aviation
3.	**T. Radheshyam Singh**	Education, Labour and Employment
4.	**Nemcha Kipgen**	Social Welfare and Cooperation
5.	**V. Hangkhalian**	Agriculture, Veterinary and Animal Husbandry
6.	**L. Jayantakumar Singh**	Health, Family Welfare, Law and Legislative, Art and Culture, CADA
7.	**Th Bishwajit Singh**	Rural Development and Panchayati Raj, Information and Public Relations, Administrative Reforms, Commerce and Industries
8.	**Letpao Haokip**	Youth Affairs, Sports, Irrigation and Flood Control
9.	**Karam Shyam**	PDS and Consumer Affairs, Weights and Measures, Revenue, Relief and Rehabilitation
10.	**N. Kayishii**	Tribal and Hill areas department and fisheries
11.	**Th Shyamkumar**	MAHUD, Forest and Environment, Horticulture, Soil Conservation and Town Planning
12.	**Loshi Dikho**	PHED, Printing and Stationary

N. Biren Singh (Honourable Chief Minister)

N. Biren Singh

Nongthombam Biren Singh (born 1 January 1961) is the current Chief Minister of Manipur. He began his career as a footballer and got recruited in the Border Security Force (BSF) playing for its team in domestic competitions. He resigned from the BSF and turned to journalism. He began the vernacular daily *Naharolgi Thoudang* in 1992 and worked as the editor till 2001.

Personal Information

Date of Birth	1 January, 1961, Luwangsangbam Mamang Leikai, Imphal East, Manipur, India
Political Party	BJP (2016-Present)
Other Political Affiliations	Indian National Congress (2003-2016), Democratic Revolutionary Peoples Party (2002-03)
Spouse(s)	Heiyainu Devi
Children	3
Alma mater	Manipur University

Politics

- In 2002, he was elected to the Legislative Assembly of Manipur, as the Democratic Revolutionary Peoples Party candidate in the constituency Heingang. He later joined the Indian National Congress.
- In May 2003, he was appointed Minister of State of Vigilance in the Manipur state government.
- In 2007, he retained his Assembly seat, contesting on behalf of the INC. He was later appointed as the Minister of Irrigation & Flood Control and Youth Affairs & Sports in the State Government.
- In 2012, he again retained his Assembly seat for the third consecutive term.
- In October 2016, Biren resigned from the Manipur Legislative Assembly and the Manipur Pradesh Congress Committee, this came after revolt against Chief Ministers of Manipur Okram Ibobi Singh.
- He formally joined the BJP on 17 October 2016 and later became the Spokesperson and Co-convener of the Election Management Committee of BJP Manipur Pradesh. He won the 2017 Manipur Legislative Assembly Election from Heingang Assembly Constituency.
- In March 2017, he was elected as leader of the BJP Legislature Party in Manipur and with a majority of MLAs having been presented to the Governor, he was sworn in as Chief Minister of Manipur on 15 March 2017. He is the first ever BJP Chief Minister in Manipur. ❑ ❑ ❑

MEMBERS OF THE MANIPUR LEGISLATIVE ASSEMBLY—ELECTIONS 2017

Name of Member	*Constituency*	*Party*
1. Thounaojam Shyamkumar*	Andro	INC
2. Konthoujam Govindas	Bishnupur	INC
3. Letpao Haokip	Chandel (ST)	NPP
4. Khashim Vashum	Chingai (ST)	NPF
5. V. Hangkhanlian	Churachandpur (ST)	BJP
6. Nongthombam Biren Singh	Heingang	BJP
7. Thokchom Radheshyam Singh	Heirok	BJP
8. T. Thangzalam Haokip	Henglep (ST)	BJP
9. Dr. Radheshyam Yumnam	Hiyanglam	BJP
10. Ashab Uddin	Jiribam	IND
11. Yengkhom Surchandra Singh*	Kakching	INC
12. Nemcha Kipgen	Kangpokpi	BJP
13. D. D. Thaisii	Karong (ST)	INC
14. Lourembam Rameshwor Meetei	Keirao	BJP
15. L. Jayantakumar Singh	Keishamthong	NPP
16. Surjakumar Okram	Khangabok	INC
17. Thokchom Lokeshwar Singh	Khundrakpam	INC
18. Leishangthem Susindro Meitei	Khurai	BJP
19. Dr. Sapam Ranjan Singh	Konthoujam	BJP
20. Nahakpam Indrajit Singh	Kshetrigao	BJP
21. Sanasam Bira Singh*	Kumbi	INC
22. Kshetrimayum Biren Singh	Lamlai	INC
23. Sorokhaibam Rajen Singh	Lamsang	BJP
24. Karam Shyam	Langthabal	LJP
25. Muhammad Abdul Nasir	Lilong	INC
26. Losii Dikho	Mao (ST)	NPF
27. Kongkham Robindro Singh	Mayang Imphal	BJP
28. Pukhrem Sharatchandra Singh	Moirang	BJP
29. Nameirakpam Loken Singh	Nambol	INC
30. Soibam Subhaschandra Singh	Naoriya Pakhanglakpa	BJP

Name of Member	Constituency	Party
31. Gaikhangam	Nungba (ST)	INC
32. Laishram Radhakishore Singh	Oinam	BJP
33. Akoijam Mirabai Devi	Patsoi	INC
34. K. Leishiyo	Phungyar (ST)	NPF
35. Rajkumar Imo Singh	Sagolband	INC
36. T. N. Haokip	Saikot (ST)	INC
37. Yamthong Haokip	Saikul (ST)	INC
38. Ngamthang Haokip*	Saitu (ST)	INC
39. Heikham Dingo Singh	Sekmai (SC)	BJP
40. Ginsuanhau*	Singhat (ST)	INC
41. Yumnam Khemchand Singh	Singjamei	BJP
42. Kangujam Ranjit Singh	Sugnu	INC
43. N. Kayisii	Tadubi (ST)	NPP
44. Awangbow Newmai	Tamei (ST)	NPF
45. Samuel Jendai Kamei	Tamenglong (ST)	BJP
46. D. Korungthang	Tengnoupal (ST)	INC
47. Tongbram Robindro Singh	Thanga	AITMC
48. Khumukcham Joykisan Singh	Thangmeiband	INC
49. Vungzagin Valte	Thanlon (ST)	BJP
50. Thongam Biswajit Singh	Thongju	BJP
51. Okram Ibobi Singh	Thoubal	INC
52. Dr. Chaltonlien Amo	Tipaimukh (ST)	INC
53. Alfred Kanngam Arthur	Ukhrul (ST)	INC
54. Yumnam Joykumar Singh	Uripok	NPP
55. Muhammad Fajur Rahim	Wabgai	INC
56. Paonam Brojen Singh	Wangjing Tentha	INC
57. Okram Henry Singh	Wangkhei	INC
58. Keisham Meghachandra Singh	Wangkhem	INC
59. Oinam Lukhoi Singh*	Wangoi	INC
60. Thokchom Satyabrata Singh	Yaiskul	BJP

* Elected on INC ticket but now in BJP.

GOVERNORS

Name	Period
Braj Kumar Nehru	21.01.1972 - 21.09.1973
Lallan Prasad Singh	21.09.1973 - 12.08.1981
Saiyid Muzaffar Hussain Burney	12.08.1981 - 02.06.1984
K.V. Krishna Rao	02.06.1984 - 01.07.1989
Chintamani Panigrahi	01.07.1989 - 20.03.1993
K.V. Raghunatha Reddy	20.03.1993 - 31.08.1993
V.K. Nayar	31.08.1993 - 23.12.1994
Oudh Narain Shrivastava	23.12.1994 - 02.12.1999
Ved Prakash Marwah	02.12.1999 - 12.06.2003
Arvind Dave	12.06.2003 - 02.08.2003
Shivinder Singh Siddhu	03.08.2003 - 23-07-2008
Gurbachan Singh Jagat	23.07.2008 - 22-07-2013
Ashwini Kumar (Add. Charge)	23.07.2013 - 31-12-2013
Vinod Kumar Duggal	31-12-2013 - 28-08-2014
K.K. Paul (Add. Charge)	29-08-2014 - 15-05-2015
Syed Ahmed	16-05-2015 - 27-09-2015
V. Shanmuganathan (Add. Charge)	28-09-2015 - 20-08-2016
Dr. Najma A. Heptulla	21-08-2016 - — —

CHIEF MINISTERS

Name	Period
Shri N. Biren Singh	15.03.2017 - — —
Shri Okram Ibobi Singh	07.03.2002 - 14.03.2017
Shri Radhabinod Koijam	15.02.2001 - 01.06.2001
Shri W. Nipamacha Singh	02.03.2000 - 14.02.2001
Shri W. Nipamacha Singh	16.12.1997 - 01.03.2000
Shri Rishang Keishing	25.02.1995 - 15.12.1997
Shri Rishang Keishing	14.12.1994 - 24.02.1995
Shri R.K. Dorendra Singh	09.04.1992 - 30.12.1993
Shri R.K. Ranbir Singh	23.02.1990 - 07.01.1992
Shri R.K. Jaichandra Singh	04.03.1988 - 17.02.1990
Shri Rishang Keishing	04.01.1985 - 04.03.1988
Shri Rishang Keishing	19.06.1981 - 04.01.1985
Shri Rishang Keishing	27.11.1980 - 28.02.1981
Shri R.K. Dorendra Singh	14.01.1980 - 26.11.1980
Shri Yangmasho Shaiza	29.06.1977 - 14.11.1979
Shri R.K. Dorendra Singh	23.07.1975 - 13.05.1977
Shri R.K. Dorendra Singh	06.12.1974 - 23.07.1975
Shri Yangmasho Shaiza	10.07.1974 - 05.12.1974
Md. Alimuddin	04.03.1974 - 08.07.1974
Md. Alimuddin	23.03.1972 - 28.03.1973
Shri M. Koireng Singh	19.02.1968 - 16.10.1969
Shri L. Thambou Singh	13.10.1967 - 25.10.1967
Shri M. Koireng Singh	20.03.1967 - 04.10.1967
Shri M. Koireng Singh	01.07.1963 - 12.01.1967
Shri M.K. Priyobrata Singh	14.08.1947 - 15.10.1949

SPEAKERS

Assembly	Name of Speaker	Period
I State Assembly (1948-49)	T.C.Tiankham	19.11.1948 to 15.10.1949
* I Territorial Council (1957-62)	1. H.Dwijamani Dev Sharma 2. Sibo Larho	Sept. 1957 to Oct.1958 Oct. 1958 to 2.8.1962
* I Territorial Assembly (1962-67)	1. M.Koireng Singh 2. Kh.Ibetombi Singh	3.8.1962 to 21.7.1963 23.7.1963 to 20.3.1967
* II Territorial Assembly (1967-69)	1. S.Tombi Singh 2. Sibo Larho	21.3.1967 to 24.10.1967 5.3.1968 to 29.3.1972
I Manipur Legislative Assembly (1972-73)	1. Dr.L.Chandramani Singh	30.3.1972 to 8.3.1974
II Manipur Legislative Assembly (1974-79)	1. R.K. Dorendra Singh 2. Md. Alimuddin 3. Dr.L.Chandramani Singh 4. R.K.Ranbir Singh	26.3.1974 to 5.12.1974 16.12.1974 to 4.9.1975 18.9.1975 to 21.10.1978 12.1.1979 to 18.2.1980
III Manipur Legislative Assembly (1980-85)	1. Y. Yaima Singh	18.2.1980 to 23.1.1985
IV Manipur Legislative Assembly (1985-90)	1. W. Angou Singh 2. Th. Devendra Singh	24.1.1985 to 20.12.1988 20.12.1988 to 2.3.1990
V Manipur Legislative Assembly (1990-95)	1. Dr. H. Borbabu Singh 2. E. Biramani Singh	2.3.1990 to 9.1.1995 9.1.1995 to 27.2.1995
VI Manipur Legislative Assembly (1995-2000)	1. W. Nipamacha Singh 2. K. Babudhon Singh	22.3.1995 to 6.12.1997 29.12.1997 to 7.3.2000
VII Manipur Legislative Assembly (2000-02)	1. Dr. S. Dhananjoy Singh	13.3.2000 to 8.3.2002
VIII Manipur Legislative Assembly (2002-2007)	1. T.N.Haokip 2. Maniruddin Sheikh	12.3.2002 to 7.12.2005 09.12.2005 to 15.3.2007
IX Manipur Legislative Assembly (2007- 2012)	1. Budhichandra Singh 2. I. Hemochandra Singh	16.3.2007 to 01.10.2010 2-10-2010 to 19-03-2012
X Manipur Legislative Assembly (2012-2017)	1. Thokchom Lokeshore	19-03-2012 to 19-03-2017
XI Manipur Legislative Assembly (2017-)	1. Y. Khemchand Singh	20-03-2017 to — —

* The nomenclature of the office of the Presiding Officer during the Territorial Council/ Territorial Assembly period is the 'Chairman'.

DEPUTY SPEAKERS

Assembly	*Name of Deputy Speaker*	*Period*
I State Assembly (1948-49)	T. Bokul Singh	19.11.1948 to 15.10.1949
I Territorial Council (1957-62)	—	—
I Territorial Assembly (1962-67)	1. L. Solomon 2. Md.Alimuddin	16.8.1963 to 15.11.1965 10.12.1965 to 12.1.1967
II Territorial Assembly (1967-69)	1. Kh.Chaoba 2. L.Ibomcha Singh	3.4.1967 to 24.10.1967 3.4.1968 to 20.10.1969
I Manipur Legislative Assembly (1972-73)	1. Atomba Ngairangbamcha	25.5.1972 to 26.3.1973
II Manipur Legislative Assembly (1974-79)	1. Th. Chaoba Singh 2. N. Paoheu 3. Ngurdinglien 4. O. Joy Singh	19.4.1974 to 30.7.1974 16.8.1974 to 10.3.1975 8.4.1975 to 16.7.1977 26.10.1977 to 14.11.1979
III Manipur Legislative Assembly (1980-85)	1. H. Lokhon Singh 2. W. Angou Singh	17.3.1980 to 14.12.1980 6.7.1981 to 4.1.1985
IV Manipur Legislative Assembly (1985-90)	1. H. Sanayaima Singh 2. M. Manihar Singh	19.2.1985 to 18.2.1990 21.3.1990 to 24.7.1990
V Manipur Legislative Assembly (1990-95)	1. N. Mangi Singh	25.9.1990 to 25.2.1995
VI Manipur Legislative Assembly (1995-00)	1. I. Hemochandra Singh 2. K. Babudhon Singh 3. Ksh. Biren Singh 4. T. T. Haokip	25.3.1995 to 28.3.1995 26.9.1995 to 27.12.1997 12.1.1998 to 7.4.1998 3.7.1998 to 1.3.2000
VII Manipur Legislative Assembly (2000-02)	1. K. Raina 2. Z. Mangaibou	6.4.2000 to 23.2.2001 23.3.2001 to 5.5.2001
VIII Manipur Legislative Assembly (2002-07)	1. K. Ranjit Singh 2. L. Lala Singh	21.3.2002 to 22.3.2002 10.7.2002 to 7.7.2004
IX Manipur Legislative Assembly (2007-2012)	1. Th. Shyam Kumar 2. Lokeshwar Singh	2-8-2007 to 18.4.2009 2009 to 18-03-2012
X Manipur Legislative Assembly (2012-2017)	1. M.K. Preshow	1-07-2013 to March 2017
XI Manipur Legislative Assembly (2017- ....)	1. K. Robindro	9-02-2018 to — —

CHAIRMEN OF HILL AREAS COMMITTEE (HAC)

Assembly	Name of Chairman	Period
I Manipur Legislative Assembly (1972-73)	1. S.P. Henry	18.10.1972 to 26.03.1973
II Manipur Legislative Assembly (1974-79)	1. Benjamin Banee 2. Saheni Adani	19.04.1974 to 03.01.1977 29.04.1977 to 13.01.1979
III Manipur Legislative Assembly (1980-85)	1. K. Huriang 2. L.S. John	17.03.1980 to 27.06.1980 11.07.1980 to 04.01.1985
IV Manipur Legislative Assembly (1985-90)	1. R.V. Mingthing 2. I.D. Dijuanang	15.03.1985 to 02.11.1988 15.11.1988 to
V Manipur Legislative Assembly (1990-95)	1. I.D. Dijuanang	24.02.1995
VI Manipur Legislative Assembly (1995-00)	1. Dr. M. Horam	02.05.1995 to 01.03.2000
VII Manipur Legislative Assembly (2000-02)	1. C. Doungel	04.04.2000 to 14.05.2001
VIII Manipur Legislative Assembly (2002-07)	1. Songchinkhup	9-4-2002 to 10-01-2007
IX Manipur Legislative Assembly (2007-2012)	Thangminlien Kipgen	13-4-2007 to 11-04-2012
X Manipur Legislative Assembly (2012-2017)	Dr. Chaltonlian Amo	12-4-2012 to 11-04-2017
XI Manipur Legislative Assembly (2017- ....)	Thangzalans Haokip	12-4-2017 to — —

MEMBERS OF LOK SABHA FROM MANIPUR

Lok Sabha Term	Constituency	Name	Party
• 1st Lok Sabha	(Inner) (Outer)	Shri Laisram Jugeswar Singh Shri Rishang Keishing	(Congress-I) (Socialist)
• 2nd Lok Sabha	(Inner) (Outer)	Shri Laisram Achaw Singh Shri Rungsung Suisa	(Socialist) (Congress-I)
• 3rd Lok Sabha	(Inner) (Outer)	Shri S. Tombi Singh Shri Rishang Keishing	(Congress-I) (Socialist)
• 4th Lok Sabha	(Inner) (Outer)	Shri M. Meghachandra Singh Shri Paokai Haokip	(CPI) (Independent)
• 5th Lok Sabha	(Inner) (Outer)	Shri N. Tombi Singh Shri Paokai Haokip	(Congress-I) (Congress-I)
• 6th Lok Sabha	(Inner) (Outer) (Outer)	Shri N. Tombi Singh Shri Yangmaso Shaiza Shri Kaiho (By-Election)	(Congress-I) (INC) (Manipur People's Party)

Lok Sabha Term	*Constituency*	*Name*	*Party*
• 7th Lok Sabha	(Inner)	Shri Ngangom Mohendra Singh	(CPI)
	(Outer)	Shri N. Gouzagin	(Congress-I)
• 8th Lok Sabha	(Inner)	Shri N. Tombi Singh	(Cogress-I)
	(Outer)	Shri Meijinlung Kamson	(Congress-I)
• 9th Lok Sabha	(Inner)	Shri N. Tombi Singh	(Congress-I)
	(Outer)	Shri Meijinlung Kamson	(Congress-I)
• 10th Lok Sabha	(Inner)	Shri Yumnam Yaima Singh	(Manipur People's Party)
	(Outer)	Prof. Meijinlung Kamson	(INC)
• 11th Lok Sabha	(Inner)	Shri Th. Chaoba Singh	(INC)
	(Outer)	Prof. Meijinlung Kamson	(INC)
• 12th Lok Sabha	(Inner)	Shri. Th. Chaoba Singh	(MSCP)
	(Outer)	Km. Kim Gangte	(CPI)
• 13th Lok Sabha	(Inner)	Shri Th. Chaoba Singh	(BJP)
	(Outer)	Shri Holkhomang Haokip	(NCP)
• 14th Lok Sabha	(Inner)	Dr. Thokchom Meinya	(INC)
	(Outer)	Shri Mani Charenamai	(Ind.)
• 15th Lok Sabha	(Inner)	Dr. Thokchom Meinya	(INC)
	(Outer)	Shri Thangso Baite	(INC)
• 16th Lok Sabha	(Inner)	Dr. Thokchom Meinya	(INC)
	(Outer)	Shri Thangso Baite	(INC)
• 17th Lok Sabha	(Inner)	Dr. Rajkumar Ranjan Singh	(BJP)
	(Outer)	Dr. Lorho S. Pfoze	(NPF)

MEMBERS OF RAJYA SABHA FROM MANIPUR

NAME	PARTY	TERM
❖ Shri Ng. Tompok Singh	INC	03.04.1954 — 02.04.1956
❖ Shri Laimayum Lalit Madhob Sharma	INC	01.12.1956 — 02.04.1960
❖ Shri Laimayum Lalit Madhob Sharma	INC	03.04.1960 — 02.11.1964
❖ Shri Sinam Krishnamohon Singh	INC	13.01.1965 — 02.04.1966
❖ Shri Sinam Krishnamohon Singh	INC	03.04.1966 — 02.04.1972
❖ Shri Salam Tombi Singh	MPP	10.04.1972 — 04.04.1974
❖ Shri Irengbam Tompok Singh	INC	18.06.1974 — 09.04.1978
❖ Shri Ng. Tompok Singh	JAN	10.04.1978 — 09.04.1984

NAME	PARTY	TERM
❖ Shri R.K. Jaichandra Singh	INC	10.04.1984 — 12.07.1988
❖ Shri R.K. Dorendra Singh	INC	20.09.1988 — 12.03.1990
❖ Shri B.D. Behring	JD	10.04.1990 — 10.04.1990*
❖ Shri W. Kulabidhu Singh	JD	13.06.1990 — 09.04.1996
❖ Shri W. Angou Singh	INC	10.04.1996 — 09.04.2002
❖ Shri Rishang Keishing	INC	10.04.2002 — 09.04.2008
❖ Shri Rishang Keishing	INC	10.04.2008 — 09-04-2014
❖ Shri Abdul Salam	INC	10.04.2014 — 28-02-2017
❖ Shri K. Bhabananda	BJP	25.05.2017 — — —

* Resigned the same day without taking oath and seat.

PRESIDENT'S RULE IN MANIPUR

	During the Presidentship of	From	To
1st time	Dr S. Radhakrishnan	12 January 1967	20 March 1967
2nd time	Dr Zakir Hussain	25 October 1967	19 February 1968
3rd time	V.V. Giri	17 October 1969	23 March 1972
4th time	V.V. Giri	28 March 1973	04 March 1974
5th time	B.D. Jatti (Acting)	16 May 1977	29 June 1977
6th time	Neelam Sanjiva Reddy	14 November 1979	14 January 1980
7th time	Neelam Sanjiva Reddy	28 February 1981	19 June 1981
8th time	R. Venkatraman	07 January 1992	08 April 1992
9th time	Dr Shankar Dayal Sharma	31 December 1993	14 December 1994
10th time	K.R. Narayanan	02 January 2001	07 March 2002

CURRENT AFFAIRS

BUDGET 2019-20

Manipur's Deputy Chief Minister, Y. Joykumar Singh, who also holds the finance portfolio, presented budget estimate for the year 2019-20 amounting to ₹ 16,117 crore in the state assembly on February 20, 2019.

Presenting the budget estimate, the finance minister said that the total fiscal deficit for the state would be ₹ 1889 crore. Increasing revenue expenditure towards salary and pension as well as interest payment against low resources makes the financial condition of the state poor, he observed. Of the ₹ 16,117 crore budget estimate, ₹ 1687 crore is charged expenditure while the remaining ₹ 14,430 is voted expenditure. Total revenue expenditure is ₹ 12,8656 crore and capital expenditure ₹ 3260 crore. The budget estimate is 22 per cent more than the gross expenditure of ₹ 13,731 crore for the year 2018-19 but ₹ 652 crore less than revised estimate of 2018-19. Joykumar observed that the state revenue is very low and 90 per cent of the gross expenditure is provided by the Central government. The state government had approved revival of state lottery in order to increase revenue resources with the projected revenue of ₹ 100 crore in the next fiscal. Despite the efforts to mobilise additional resources, the state would continue to face fund constraints in the years to come, he said. The budget estimate gives special emphasis on education, health, water resources, urban development, agriculture, forest and rural development. An amount of ₹ 25 crore has been earmarked for Go to School mission and ₹ 50 lakh for cash incentives to toppers of HSLCE and HSE. Another amount of ₹ 6 crore has been earmarked for Dhanamanjuri University, he told the House.

In the health sector, ₹ 20 crore has been earmarked for the state government's flagship programme 'Chief Ministergi Hakshelgi Tengbang'. Agriculture sector contributes 52.8 per cent of the state's total workforce and has been the backbone of the state's economy. Unfortunately, the government has been unable to provide appropriate irrigation facilities to more than 60 per cent of the total agricultural land of the state, Joykumar said, adding that ₹ 438 crore has been earmarked to improve irrigation networks. On the other hand, AIBP fund for fighting flood calamities has been increased to ₹ 221 crore, the finance minister said. Regarding urban development, Joykumar said that the government has earmarked ₹ 614 crore for urban infrastructure, urban poverty, urban planning and employment generation besides another ₹ 8 crore for developing civic amenities. A fund of ₹ 788 crore has been earmarked for improving conditions of ST, SC, OBC and minorities, he said. On the other hand, the state government is seeking a fund of Rs 316 crore from the Centre for different schemes and missions in the agriculture sector. An amount of ₹ 6.28 crore has also been earmarked for adequate stocking of urea fertilisers, he added.

The budget allocation for national bamboo mission and Green India Mission has been increased to ₹ 232 crore from the last fiscal's ₹ 192 crore. An amount of ₹ 20 crore has been earmarked for watershed management for Singda Dam, Thoubal River and Imphal River under EAP. The government is looking forward to cut down unnecessary expenditures and increase capital expenditures. Large scale recruitment in 2016-17 affects the expenditure management especially in revenue expenditure of the state. There is projection of 31.44 per cent increased expenditure for salary and pension than that of 2017-18, the deputy CM said. The recent hike of DA, DR for government employees and adoption of 7th Central Pay Commission will also have major impact in the revenue expenditure, which will increase the fiscal deficit. The government had submitted a presentation to the 15th Finance Commission in this regard and the state government has firm belief that the commission will approve the proposal of the state, Joykumar added.

In his concluding remarks, the finance minister stated that no budget can be the panacea for all the disadvantages which a society faces. "However, it is our earnest hope that the budget shall bring at least some incremental positive changes to the lives of the people. The budget is not just an economic intent but is also a vehicle to express the seriousness of the government towards the holistic development of the state," he added.

PM INAUGURATED 12 PROJECTS

On January 4, 2019, Prime Minister, Narendra Modi was on a day long visit to Imphal, Manipur. He inaugurated 12 projects worth over ₹ 1500 crore.

Addressing a public gathering, he inaugurated 12 projects consisting of eight key development projects related to water supply and tourism and four schemes in Manipur. These include:

- An Integrated Check Post at Moreh, Imphal, at a cost of over ₹ 125 crore, that will facilitate custom clearance, foreign currency exchange, immigration clearance etc,
- The Dolaithabi Barrage Project which completed at a total cost of ₹ 500 crore,
- The FCI Food Storage Godown at Sawombung that had begun in December 2016,
- He dedicated to the nation the 400 kV Double Circuit Silchar-Imphal Line that was made at a cost of ₹ 700 crore.
- A buffer water reservoir at Ukhrul was mentioned which would be helping the citizens till 2035,
- He inaugurated improved and upgraded water supply for Churachandpur zone which will help the citizens till 2031,

- Eco-tourism complex at Thangapat in Kangpokpi district,
- Integrated tourist destination in Noney district and
- The water supply scheme at JNV, Lambui and its surrounding villages
- Infrastructure development of Dhanamanjuri University in Imphal West district,
- Flood lighting of hockey stadium and the main stadium at the Khuman Lampak Sports Complex in Imphal East district and
- AstroTurf laying in Langjing Achouba of Imphal West district.

MANIPUR YOUTH INDUCTED INTO FACEBOOK 'HALL OF FAME'

A 22-year-old civil engineer, Zonel Sougaijam from Imphal east of Manipur was recognized by the social media giant "Facebook" for discovering and reporting a WhatsApp bug that violated the privacy of a user. Zonel Sougaijam was rewarded $5000 and also inducted into the Facebook 'Hall of Fame' 2019. Now he is at the 16th position in a rundown of 94 people in the 'Facebook Hall of Fame' 2019. The bug bounty program of Facebook where the user can report critical bugs which violates the privacy of its users.

NEW MEDICINAL PLANTS DISCOVERED IN MANIPUR

New medicinal plants of Zeliangrong ethnic group were found in Manipur by the research team from North Eastern Regional Institute of Sciences and Technology, Arunachal Pradesh. This study was published in the Journal of Ethnopharmacology. The lead author of the study was Robert Panmei and the members were P. R. Gajurela and B. Singh. Zeliangrong ethnic group is one of the 32 tribes in Manipur, living in the Tamenglong district. It comprises of three groups namely Zeme, Liangmai and Rongmei which are collectively known as Zeliangrong. 27 healers of the Zeliangrong ethnic group were examined and the researchers documented 145 medicinal plants for treating 59 ailments. Scientists identified plants like Gynura cusimbua, Hedyotis scandens, Mussaenda glabra, and Schima wallichii whose medicinal usage was reported for the first time. The study was conducted with the consent of the community as per the code of ethics of the International Society of Ethnobiology (ISE).

FORMER MINISTER HOLKHOMANG HAOKIP PASSED AWAY

Holkhomang Haokip, veteran politician and former minister of Manipur passed away on 8th April 2019.Holkhomang Haokip was a leader of the Kuki community (of North-east India) and being elected to the 13th Lok Sabha (in 1999). He was a former member of Parliament. He hailed from Kamjong District of Manipur. Holkhomang Haokip was the son of freedom fighter Chunglet Haokip of the (INA) Indian National Army. Previously, in 1972, he was elected to the Manipur Assembly and became the minister of Manipur for education and tribal welfare. Haokip was appointed as the deputy chairman of the State Planning Board in 1980. iv. From 1981 to 1984, Haokip was a cabinet minister of industries, planning and transport. From 1989 to 1992 he was the industry minister and from 1992 to 1995, the power Minister.

PHAYENG VILLAGE TAGGED AS INDIA'S FIRST CARBON-POSITIVE SETTLEMENT

On 1st April 2019, Phayeng, a scheduled caste village of the Chakpa community in Imphal West district of Manipur has been tagged as India's first carbon-positive settlement. The village is surrounded by three densely forested hillocks with fruit trees at centre and a stream flowing through it. Also, it has been revived from the dry and denuded village through the sheer determination of its residents and funding under National Adaptation Fund for Climate Change (NAFCC), which is a central scheme launched in 2015-16 to support adaptation for climate change impact in various states.

NAMKAOBI KAMEI RECEIVES ELEVEN PRESTIGIOUS AWARDS

Namkaobi Kamei, a physician and cultivator from Namkaolong (Keikao) village under Tamenglong sub- Division of Tamenglong district has received at least eleven prestigious awards from Friendship Forum of India in February, 2019. Namkaobi Kamei had attended a conference on "Economic Growth and National Unity" at New Delhi held on February 24, 2019 which was organised by Friendship Forum of India. During the conference, he was conferred the "India's Leading Global Healing Institution Award 2019", "Acharya Ratan Award 2019", "India's Most Admired Personality Award 2019", "Leading North Eastern Golden Personality Award 2019", "Global Arch of Excellence Award 2019" and "International Man of the Year Award 2019" which came along with gold medals, certificates and mementos.

MANIPUR
General Knowledge

MANIPUR : A PROFILE

The word "Manipur" is being derived from the two Sanskrit Words "Mani" and "Pur", which literally mean 'A Jewelled Land' or 'The Land of Jewels'. Here "Mani" means Jewel and "Pur" means land or place respectively.

Surrounded by blue hills with an oval shaped valley at the centre, rich in art and tradition and surcharged with nature's pristine glory, Manipur lies on a melting pot of culture. It is birth place of Polo. This is the place where Rajashree Bhagyachandra created the famous Ras Lila, the classical dance of Manipur, out of his enchanting dream by the grace of Lord Krishna. Her folk dances reveal the mythological concept of creation of Manipur.

Having a varied and proud history from the earliest times, Manipur came under the British Rule as a Princely State after the defeat in the Anglo-Manipuri War of 1891. After independence of India in 1947, the Princely State of Manipur was merged in the Indian Union on October 15,1949 and became a full-fledged State of India on the 21th January, 1972 with a Legislative Assembly of 60 seats of which 19 are reserved for Scheduled Tribe and one reserved for Scheduled Caste. The State is represented in the Lok Sabha by two members and by one member in the Rajya Sabha.

Manipur extends between 23°50' and 25°42' latitudes north and between 92°58' and 94°45' longitudes east. It covers an area of 22,327 square kilometers and is bounded on the north by Nagaland, on the west by Cachar of Assam, on the east by Burma (Myanmar) and on the south by Mizoram and Chin state of Burma.

IMPORTANT FACTS

Capital	:	Imphal
Area	:	22327 sq.km.
Population (2011 Census)	:	28,55,794 (*Males*: 14,38,586; *Females*: 14,17,208)
Decadal Growth Rate	:	24.50%
Density of Population	:	128 (per sq. km.)
Literacy Rate	:	76.94%
Sex Ratio	:	985 (Females per 1000 Males)

Altitude	:	790 mtrs. above MSL (Imphal)
Latitude	:	23°50'N to 25°42'N
Longitude	:	92°58'E to 94°45'E
Rainfall	:	1467.5 mm (Avg.)
Rainy Season	:	May to October
Climate		
Summer	:	14°C to 32°C
Winter	:	0°C to 25°C
State Language	:	Manipuri
State Emblem	:	Kangla Sha
State Bird	:	Nongyeen
State Animal	:	Sangai
State Game	:	Manipuri Polo
State Flower	:	Siroi Lily
State Tree	:	Uning thou
Assembly Constituencies	:	60
Parliamentary Constituencies	:	2 (One for Inner and One for Outer)
Rajya Sabha Seat	:	1
National Highways	:	3(NH-39-Indo-Myanmar road, NH-53-New Cachar Road, NH-150-Jessami-Tipaimukh Road)
Districts	:	16-Senapati, Tamenglong, Thoubal, Ukhrul, Bishnupur, Chandel, Churachandpur, Imphal East, Imphal West, Jiribam, Kangpokpi, Kakching, Tengnoupal, Kamjong, Noney, Pherzawl.
Sub-divisions	:	66
Towns	:	51 *(Statutory towns 28, Census towns 23)*
Small Town Committees	:	33
Gram Panchayats	:	165
Largest District	:	Churachandpur
Smallest District	:	Bishnupur
Highly Populated District (2011)	:	Imphal West
Less Populated District	:	Tamenglong
Most Densily Populated District (2011)	:	Imphal West (998 persons per sq. km.)
Less populated District (2011)	:	Tamenglong (32 persons per sq. km)

Major Religions	: Hinduism, Christianity, Maibiasn
Major Festivals	: Rath Yatra, Yaoshang (Dol Jatra), Christmas, Diwali, ID, Mahavir Jayanti, Lai Haraoba, Kut, Gan-Ngai, Cheiraoba
Major Cities	: Imphal, Churachandpur, Kakching, Ukhrul, Andro, Bishnupur, Jiribam, Moirang, Moreh, Ningthoukhong, Thoubal, etc.
Largest City	: Imphal
Major Tourist Places	: Shaheed Minar, War Cemetery, Manipur Zoological Garden, Keibul Lamjao National Park, Kaina, Red Hill (Maibam Lok pa Ching), Loukoipat, Shree Shree Govindajee Temple, Phubala, Loktak Lake, Leimaram, Moreh, Tengnoupal, Andro, Khongjom, etc.
Major Crops	: Wheat, Rice, Pulses, Paddy, Maize, Sugarcane, Potato, Mustard, etc.
Major Fruits	: Pineapple, Banana, Papaya, Passion Fruit, Orange, Lemon, Mango etc.
Major Vegetables	: Cabbage, Cauliflower, Peas, French Beans, Tomato, etc.
Major Spices	: Green Chilli, Ginger, Turmeric, Corriander Seeds, etc.
Major Forest Products	: Oak, Teak, Pine, Cane, Bamboo, Leihao, Uningthou, etc.
Major Import Products	: Betel nut, Silk yarn, Pigs, Cotton thread, etc.
Major Export Products	: Bamboo shoot products (orient food), ginger, pineapple, Maize, Mushrooms, etc.
Chief Rivers	: Barak, Imphal, Khuga, Maklang, Ithai, Thoubal, Irang, Nambul, Chakpi, Sekmai, etc.
Major Minerals	: Copper, Nickel, Chromite, Asbestos, Limestone, Lignite, etc.

ADMINISTRATION

Manipur in its wide territory of 22,327 sq. km. includes 16 districts. The name of districts are Imphal-East, Imphal-West, Senapati, Tamenglong, Thoubal, Ukhrul, Bishnupur, Chandel, Churachandpur, Jiribam, Kangpokpi, Kakching, Tengnoupal, Kamjong, Noney and Pherzawl. Number of Sub-divisions (2018) is 66. For the upliftment and development of the rural areas, the state is sub-divided into 34 community and Tribal Development Blocks and 33 small town committees. The Manipur Legislative Assembly consists of 60 seats out of which, 19 seats are reserved for scheduled Tribes, 1 for Scheduled Caste and 40 for General. Manipur has a two-tier panchayati Raj system. Gram Panchayat at the Village level and the Zila Parishad at the district level. There are about 165 Gram Panchayats and 4 Zila Parishads (the Imphal East Zila Parishad, the Imphal West Zila Parishad, the Thoubal Zila Parishad and the Bishnupur Zila Parishad) in Manipur.

Manipur sends 2 members to Lok-Sabha (Lower House of the Indian Parliament) and 1 member to the Rajya Sabha (Upper House of the Indian Parliament). Manipur was within the jurisdiction of the Imphal Bench of Gauhati High Court till March 25, 2013. Earlier, the Imphal Bench of Gauhati High Court came into existence on 21st January, 1972, the day Manipur attained its statehood. In March 2013, the then Chief Justice of India Altamas Kabir formally inangurated the Manipur High Court at Imphal and Justice Abhay Manohar Sapre was made the first Chief Justice of the Manipur High Court.

DISTRICTS AND SUB-DIVISIONS OF MANIPUR

Sl. No.	Name of District	Name of Sub-division
1.	**Senapati**	1. Tadubi
		2. Paomata
		3. Purul
		4. Willong
		5. Chilivai Phaibung
		6. Song-Song
		7. Lairouching

Sl. No.	Name of District	Name of Sub-division
2.	**Kangpokpi** (Bifurcated from the erstwhile Senapati District)	8. Kangpokpi
		9. Champhai
		10. Saitu Gamphazol
		11. Kangchup Geljang
		12. Tuijang Waichong
		13. Saikul
		14. Lungtin
		15. Island
		16. Bungte Chiru
3.	**Tamenglong**	17. Tamenglong
		18. Tamei
		19. Tousem
4.	**Noney District** (Bifurcated from the erstwhile Tamenglong District)	20. Nungba
		21. Khoupum
		22. Longmei (Noney)
		23. Haochong
5.	**Churachandpur**	24. Churachandpur
		25. Sangaikot
		26. Tuibuong
		27. Mualnuam
		28. Singngat
		29. Henglep
		30. Kangvai
		31. Samulamlan
		32. Saikot
6.	**Pherzawl** (Bifurcated from the erstwhile Churachandpur District)	33. Pherzawl
		34. Thanlon
		35. Parbung-Tipaimukh
		36. Vangai Range
7.	**Chandel**	37. Chandel
		38. Chakpikarong
		39. Khengjoy
8.	**Tengnoupal District** (Bifurcated from the erstwhile Chandel District)	40. Machi
		41. Moreh
		42. Tengnoupal

Sl. No.	Name of District	Name of Sub-division
9.	**Ukhrul**	43. Ukhrul
		44. Lungchong-Maiphai
		45. Chingai
		46. Jessami
10.	**Kamjong District** (Bifurcated from the erstwhile Ukhrul District)	47. Kamjong
		48. Sahamphung
		49. Kasom Khullen
		50. Phungyar
11.	**Imphal East**	51. Porompat
		52. Keirao Bitra
		53. Sawombung
12.	**Jiribam** (Bifurcated from the erstwhile Imphal East District)	54. Jiribam
		55. Borobekra
13.	**Imphal West**	56. Lamshang
		57. Patsoi
		58. Lamphelpat
		59. Wangoi
14.	**Bishnupur**	60. Nambol
		61. Bishnupur
		62. Moirang
15.	**Thoubal District**	63. Thoubal
		64. Lilong
16.	**Kakching** (Bifurcated from the erstwhile Thoubal District)	65. Kakching
		66. Waikhong

MUNICIPALITY

In Manipur there are altogether 9 municipalities which is headed by the Municipality Commission.

Sl.No.	Name of Municipal	Total No. of Ward
1.	Imphal Municipal Council	27
2.	Kakching Municipal Council	12

Sl.No.	Name of Municipal	Total No. of Ward
3.	Thoubal Municipal Council	18
4.	Jiribam Municipal Council	10
5.	Moirang Municipal Council	12
6.	Bishnupur Municipal Council	12
7.	Nambol Municipal Council	18
8.	Mayang Imphal Municipal Council	13
9.	Ningthoukhong Municipal Council	

NAGAR PANCHAYATS

There are 18 Nagar Panchayats in the state.

Sl. No.	Name of Nagar Panchayats	Total No. of Ward	Sl. No.	Name of Nagar Panchayats	Total No. of Ward
1.	Andro	12	10.	Heirok	12
2.	Lilong (Thoubal)	9	11.	Wangjing Lamding	9
3.	Lamshang	9	12.	Shikhong Sekmai	3
4.	Wangoi	12	13.	Yairipok	9
5.	Lamlai	9	14.	Sugnu	9
6.	Sekmai	9	15.	Oinam	9
7.	Thongkhong Laxmi Bazar	11	16.	Kakching Khunou	9
8.	Lilong (Imphal West)	9	17.	Kumbi	9
9.	Samurou	12	18.	Kwakta	9

ADMINISTRATION OF MANIPUR : AT A GLANCE

- Number of Districts (2018) : 16
- Number of Sub-divisions (2018) : 66
- Autonomous Hill District Council (2018) : 6
- Legislature : Unicameral
- Assembly Seats : 60 (19 for Scheduled Tribes; 1 for Scheduled Castes and 40 for General).
- MP sent to Lok Sabha : 2
- MP sent to Rajya Sabha : 1
- Community and Tribal Development Blocks : 34
- Number of Towns : 51 *(Statutory towns 28, Census towns 23)*
- Small Town Committees : 33
- Number of Municipalities in the urban areas of Manipur : 9 (2 in the hill areas and 7 in the valley areas)
- Gram Panchayats : 165
- Zila Parishads : 4 (the Imphal East Zila Parishad, the Imphal West Zila Parishad, the Thoubal Zila Parishad and the Bishnupur Zila Parishad).

AUTONOMOUS DISTRICT COUNCIL

The Manipur (Hill Areas) District Council Act, 1971, an Act passed by the Parliament paved the way for establishment of six Autonomous District Councils in Manipur. In accordance with the powers vested on the Governor of Manipur, following six Autonomous Districts Councils were constituted on 14th February, 1972 :

1. Churachandpur ADC
2. Chandel ADC
3. Senapati ADC
4. Sadar Hills ADC
5. Tamenglong ADC
6. Ukhrul ADC

The first election to the autonomous district councils was held in 1973.

Amendments to the Act: So far the 1971 Act has been amended thrice:

1975 : The first amendment to the Act envisaged removal of the Chairman of the District Council by the Government for reasons to be recorded in writing upon passing of a resolution by the District Council by a simple majority of the total membership of the Council.

2006 : The second amendment envisaged the following features:

- Notifying areas as urban areas for the purpose of development plan and to execute the works;
- Allotment/transfer/lease of land by a resolution passed by the District Council.

2008 : The third amendment to the Act envisaged the following:

- Increase in membership from 18 to 24.
- Election Commission of the State to be entrusted election to HDC;
- Constitution of Executive Committee.
- Addition of 9 entries to the list of powers of the autonomous Hill Districts.

HISTORY

PERIODS IN THE HISTORY OF MANIPUR

A careful study of a language may reveal a considerable amount of the historical events, the origin, migration, the art and culture of the people. Sir William Jones, a British judge in India in 1786 while studying the Sanskrit literature revealed that it bears a striking resemblance with other two ancient languages — Latin and Greek. The Sanskrit word for father 'Pitar' is astonishingly similar to the Greek and Latin 'Pater'. Similarly, Sanskrit 'Matar' Latin and Greek 'Mater' and English 'Mother' and Hindi 'Mata' share a considerable affinity. Two hundred years of linguistic research had provided evidences that one-third of the human race might have come from this Indo-European "common source", probably between 3500-2500 BC in the central Europe, from where people migrated to the West and East.

In case of the Meitei people, since there were no modern system of recording, where the sense of originality was always contemplated with the modern history, the reconstruction of the ancient manuscripts and languages has yielded a considerable knowledge on the history of ancient Manipur. The following is a brief history or Puwari of some prominent Meitei rulers with a view to bring out an understanding of the various developments in Meitei history, art, culture, tradition, sports, etc. The account is not complete but hope to provide an overall grasp on the history of Manipur.

The history of Manipur may be divided into four main periods: (i) **The Ancient period** (before Christ), (ii) **The early period** (1st-13th AD), (iii) **The Medieval period** (15-18th AD) and (iv) **The Modern period** (19-20th Century AD).

PRESENT MANIPUR

On 21 January 1972, Manipur was granted Statehood after several years of demand by All Manipur Students Union and several political organisations. The ceremony was performed at the Palace Polo ground in Imphal. In 1992, Meitei-lon (Manipuri) was included in the Eighth Schedule as one of the 22 official languages of India. Manipur has yet to see a proper road connection to the rest of India. Air transportations are provided from Kolkata, New Delhi, Gauhati and Silchar but much beyond the reach of commoners.

FAMOUS TITLES OF WELL KNOWN PERSONS

TITLE	NAME
❖ The Lion of Manipur	: Bir Tikendrajit
❖ Mahakavi	: Hijam Anganghal
❖ Melody King	: Nongmaithem Pahari
❖ Melody Queen	: Smt. Laishram Mema Devi
❖ Tarzan of Manipur	: Irom Leikhendra
❖ Bob	: Ralengnao Kathing
❖ Jananeta (leader of the people)	: Hijam Irabot
❖ Kaksu	: Meidigu Tonkonba
❖ Agayestha of the East	: Atombapu Sharma
❖ Thangal General	: Kangabam Chitananda Singha
❖ Leipok Keirungba	: Leimapokpam Dev Singh

KINGS OF MANIPUR

Name	Period of reign (A.D.)	Number of Years / Months
❖ Nongda Lairen Pakhangba	33-154	121
❖ Khuiyoi Tompok	154-264	110
❖ Taothingmang	264-364	100
❖ Khui Ningonba	364-379	15
❖ Pengsiba	379-394	15
❖ Kaokhangba	394-411	17
❖ Naokhamba	411-428	17
❖ Naophangba	428-518	90
❖ Sameirang	518-568	50
❖ Wura Konthouba	568-658	90
❖ Naothingkhong	663-763	100
❖ Khongtekcha	763-773	10
❖ Keirencha	784-799	15
❖ Yaraba	799-821	22
❖ Ayangba	821-910	89
❖ Ningthoucheng	910-949	39
❖ Chenglie-Ipan-Lanthaba	949-969	20
❖ Keiphaba Yanglon	969-984	15
❖ Irengba	984-1074	90
❖ Loiyumba	1074-1112	48
❖ Loitongba	1122-1150	28

Name	Period of reign (A.D.)	Number of Years / Months
❖ Atom Yoiremba	1150-1163	13
❖ Iyanthaba	1163-1195	32
❖ Thayanthaba	1195-1231	36
❖ Chingthang Lanthaba	1231-1242	11
❖ Thingbai Shelhongba	1242-1247	5
❖ Puranthaba	1247-1263	16
❖ Khumomba	1263-1278	15
❖ Moiramba	1278-1302	24
❖ Thangbi Lanthaba	1302-1324	22
❖ Kongyamba	1324-1335	11
❖ Telheiba	1335-1355	20
❖ Tonaba	1355-1359	4
❖ Tabungba	1339-1394	35
❖ Lairenba	1394-1399	5
❖ Punsiba	1404-1432	28
❖ Ningthoukhomba	1432-1467	35
❖ Kyamba	1467-1508	41
❖ Koiremba	1508-1512	4
❖ Lamkhyamba	1512-1523	11
❖ Nonginphaba	1523-1524	1
❖ Kabomba	1524-1542	18
❖ Tangjamba	1542-1545	3
❖ Chalamba	1545-1562	17
❖ Mugyamba	1562-1597	35
❖ Khagemba	1597-1652	55
❖ Khunjaoba	1652-1666	14
❖ Paikhomba	1666-1697	31
❖ Charairongba	1697-1709	12
❖ Garibniwaj	1709-1748	39
❖ Chitshai	1748-1752	4
❖ Bharatsai	1752-1753	1
❖ Maramba	1753-1759	6
❖ Chingthangkhomba	1759-1762	3
❖ Maramba	1762-1763	1
❖ Chingthangkhomba	1763-1798	35
❖ Labanyachandra	1798-1801	3
❖ Madhuchandra	1801-1803	2
❖ Chourjit	1803-1813	10

Name	Period of reign (A.D.)	Number of Years / Months
❖ Marjit	1813-1819	6
❖ Takuningthou (Herachandra)	1819	1
❖ Yumjaotaba	1820	1
❖ Gambhir Singha	1821	6 months
❖ Jai Singha	1822	1
❖ Jadu Singha (Nongpok Chinslenkhomba)	1823	1
❖ Raghab Singha	1823-1824	1
❖ Nongchup Lamgaingamba (Bhadrasing)	1824	1
❖ Gambhir Singha (Chinglen Nongdrenkhomba)	1825-1834	9
❖ Chandrakirti (Ningthempishak)	1834-1844	10
❖ Nara Singha	1844-1850	6
❖ Debendra Singha	1850	3 months
❖ Chandrakirti (K.C.S.I.)	1850-1886	36
❖ Surchandra	1886-1890	4
❖ Kulachandra	1890-1891	1
❖ Churachand Singha	1891-1941	50
❖ Bodhachandra Singha	1941-1955	14

IMPORTANT DATES IN MANIPUR HISTORY

33 A.D. – The first king of Manipur was Pakhangba who reigned for 120 years.

154 A.D. – Khuiyoi Tompok ascended the throne and it is belived that during his reign 'Pung' (drum) was first invented.

264 A.D. – Taothing Mang ascended the throne.

568 – Wura Konthouba become a King.

1074 – King Loiyumba came to the throne during his reign many social reform took place.

1247 – Puranthaba became King and in his reign chinese invaded Manipur but was defeated.

1404 – Luwang Punsiba, who introduced the international game of Polo for the first time on the soil of Manipur, ascended the throne.

1467 – Kyamba, who was noted for his military and administration achievement ascended the throne.

1597	–	Khangemba become a King and introduced first Manipur coins.
1704	–	King Charairongba was initial into Vaishnavism with the result that Vaishnavism become state religion.
1714	–	Garibaniwaj ascended the throne.
1736	–	Garibaniwaj again with an army crossed Ningthee river and attacked and destroyed the town of Meyedu, on the bank of Yu river.
1762	–	The first Alliance become Manipur and East India Company was made.
1765	–	The second Burmese invasion took place.
1775	–	Occurance of the worst flood known as 'Wang Khem Echao'.
1776	–	Set-up the Govindajee Temple at Imphal by king Bheigyachandra.
1819	–	'Seven year Disertation' 1819 to 1825, Magazine wore a deserted look under the tyrancy of invading Burmese.
1826	–	Making of the "Treaty of Yandaboo".
1833	–	Annexation of Jiribam to Manipur during the reign of Gambir Singh.
1834	–	The Kabaw Valley was handed over to Burma.
1885	–	First English school was established.
1891	–	The Government of India under the British declared war against Manipur; Yuvaraj Tikendrajit and General Thangal were executed by hanging at Pheida Pung (Present B.T. Park).
1904	–	First Nupeelal (Women's war against British)
1907	–	Manipur State Darbar was established to assist the Maharaja in the administration of Manipur.
1931	–	The hanging of Jadonang who was a great Zeliangrong leader.
1939	–	Nupeelal, i.e. Second Women's war against the misrule of the British and it continued for about 14 months.
1941	–	Maharaj Bodhachandra become the king of Manipur by succeeding to his father Chura Chand.
1944	–	The INA Flag Hoisted at Moirang.
1949	–	Merger agreement was signed between the government of India and Manipur.
1957	–	Manipur become one of the Union Territories under the Union Territories Act, 1956.
1960	–	Panchayati Raj System was introduced in Manipur.

1963 – A Legislative assembly of 30 elected and 3 nominated was established under the Govt. of Union Territory Act, 1963; The AIR station of Imphal was inaugurated.
1967 – President's Rule was imposed for the first time in Manipur.
1972 – Manipur became a full fledged state.
1980 – The Manipur university was established.
1987 – TV transmission centre was opened.
1992 – Manipur Language have included in the 8th Schedule of the Constitution of India by the 71st Amendment of Constitution.
1995 – DD-2 metro channel of DDK-Imphal was opened.
1997 – Divided the Imphal East & Imphal West District.
1999 – The 5th National Games were held in Manipur. Manipur overall champion.
2000 – Manipur Cup 2000, 5th International Invitation Polo Tournament at Imphal win Manipur Polo Team.
2002 – The President of India APJ Abdul Kalam, inaugurated the 36 MW Heavey fuel based Power plant at Leimakhong, 20 Km from Imphal.
2004 – Prime Minister Dr. Manmohan Singh handed over the Kangla Fort to the government of India.
2005 – The first Chief Minister of Manipur M.K. Priyobrata passess away at his residence located in Konung Leikei at Palace Compound, Imphal.
2006 – Former Chief Minister of Manipur R.K. Ranabir Singh passes away at his residence at Keishamthong Longiam Leirak, Imphal.
2007 – Manipur gets second position in 33rd National Games held in Guwahati (February 9-18) with 51 gold, 32 silver and 40 bronze medals.
2008 – The Manipur government has decided to construct 25 residential schools in the state with funding from the centre.
2009 – Boxing icon M.C. Mary kom awarded with Rajiv Gandhi Khel Ratna award for 2008-09.
2010 – Manipur won 18th Senior National Women's Football tournament.
2011 – Manipur won Best State Award in 34th National Games-2011.
2012 – Boxing icon M.C. Mary Kom won bronze medal in 2012 London Olympics.
2013 – Chief Justice of India Altamas Kabir inaugurated the Manipur High Court on March 25, 2013.
2014 – Seven Sportspersons from Manipur won medals (3 Gold and 4 Bronze) in Asian Games–2014 held in Incheon, South Korea.
2015 – Binalakshmi Nepram wins L'oreal Paris Femina Women Awards 2015.
2016 – Maurice Yengkhom and Chongtham Kuber Meitei got National Bravery Award; M.C. Mary Kom nominated in Rajya Sabha.
2017 – BJP leader N. Biren Singh became new CM of Manipur.
2018 – The Union Cabinet approved the ordinance of setting India's first National Sports University in Imphal.
2019 – Ms. Bombayla Devi Laishram (Sports–Archery) got Padma Shri.

THE ANGLO-MANIPUR WAR 1891

The war of Independence or the Anglo- Manipur War 1891, makes an epoch in the history of Manipur. This historic war started initially due to the manual jealously, dissension, distrust and discord amongst the princes of Manipur. After the death of maharaja Chandrakirti Singh, his eldest son Surchandra succeeded to the throne in the year 1886. Since the ascendence of Surchandra Singh, the royal family of Manipur divided into two factions viz., on one side Jubaraj Kullachandra, Tikendrajit, Angousana and Zillanamba joined against the king. The discord between the brothers had been going on for quite sometime but was made public on September 21st,1890 (the palace revolt). Surchandra and his three brothers rushed to Calcutta and appealed to the British Govt. for help. In the meantime Kullachandra became the king and Tikendrajit became the Jubraj of Manipur. Taking advantage of the internal dissension of the royal family, the British Government openly interfered in the administration of Manipur. As a matter of fact, the British Government wanted to keep Manipur under their control from the very beginning.

They had enough time to poison the minds of the princes by hatching a deep-roosted controversy in order to accomplish their nefarious goal.

After an interview between Lord Landsdowne, the Viceroy of India and Mr. J.W. Quinton, Chief Commissioner of Assam on 21st Feburary 1891, the following decisions were arrived at:-

(1) Removal of Senapati Tikendrajit from Manipur.
(2) Recognizing Regent Kullachandra as Maharaja and
(3) Making known the decision by personal visit of Quinton to Manipur.

The Chief Commissioner Mr. J.W. Quinton arrived to Manipur on 22nd March, 1891. He was received by Tikendrajit and Thangal General with a guard of honour by the Manipuri troops. Truly speaking, Mr. Quinton's visit to Manipur with his misguided mission became a very important cause for the Anglo-Manipur war, 1891. Mr. Quinton and his party led to the massacre of their objective to capture Tikendrajit Singh.

The sons of Manipur fought against the British for their motherland. Many heroes like Yaiskul Lakpa, Chinglensana, Brajabasi Paona and Mairaba etc. sacrificed their lives. On 27th April, 1891 the British hoisted their flag at Kangla (now the Assam Rifles area). From this day onwards, the Manipuris were under the direct control of the British.

HEROS OF MANIPUR'S WAR OF INDEPENDENCE

JUBRAJ TIKENDRAJIT SINGH : Jubraj Tikendrajit Singh, the hero of the Manipur revolution of 1891, was born in 1858. He was the son of Maharaja Chandrakirti Singh and his mother's name was Chongtham Chanu Kouseswari Devi.

During the reign of his father (Maharaja Chandrakriti), he was Kotwal, Senapati (during the period of Surachandra) and Jubraj (during the period of Kullachandra). In his individual capacity, he deposed Surchandra, the reigning king in the year 1890 and installed Kullachandra as the king of Manipur. The rise of such a powerful prince in the eastern most state of India was considered as a threat to the British Supremacy and the Britishes decided to "chopping the fall popy". Lord Landsdowne regarded this act of indiscretion on the part of Tikendrajit as a great offence. It also gave an opportunity to the British to interfere in the internal affairs of Manipur. He determined to expel the British from Manipur and bring back her independence. Mr. Quinton arrived in Manipur on 22nd March, 1891and he asked the Raja to hand over Tikendrajit to him as desired by the Governor General of India. This led to a direct clash of arms between the Manipuris and the British. In course of the Skirmish, which took place in the palace campus, Quinton himself, with a number of his officers were put to death. On receipt of this news the British Government sent three columns of troops to Manipur from Kohima, Silchar and Tamu. To save their motherland, the Manipuris fought very bravely under the direction of Tikendrajit. But it was all in vain against the superior mite and arms of the British. On 27th April, 1891 the British occupied Manipur. Tikendrajit was arrested and after a farcical trial by a general court-martial, he was publicly hanged at Pheida Pung presently B.T. Park on 13th August 1891.

Some other influencing personalities of Manipur's War of Independence are:

- General Thangal
- Kajao alias Pukhramba
- Maharaja Kulachandra Dhaja (Ex-Regent)
- Lokendra Birjit Singh, Wangkheirakpa
- Chongtham Nilamani Singh
- Uru Singh, Usurba
- Ghun Singh, Kongdram
- Dhaja Singh, Mayengba
- Trilok Singh, Nongtholba Satwal
- Ghun Singh
- Thaoba Singh
- Chaobatol Singh, Heigrujamba
- Niranjan Subadar
- Chirai Nagas Alias Chirai Thangal
- Prince Angou Sana Senapati
- Samu Singh, Colonel
- Chongtha Mia Singh, Major
- Chauba Hida Machahal
- Kumba Singh, Laishramba
- Nam Singh, Nepra Machahal
- Dhon Singh
- Ningthouba Singh
- Tonjao Singh
- Paradhumba Singh

GEOGRAPHY

Manipur has a total surface area of 22,327 sq. km. forming 0.7% of the total land surface of the Indian Union. It is situated between the parallels 23°50'N -25°42'N and the meridians 92°58'E - 94°45'E. It has a border of 854 km of which 352 km is international border with Myanmar on the east. The remaining 502 km long border separates her from the neighboring states of Nagaland on the north, Assam on the west and Mizoram on the south and the south west. Physiographically the land is divisible into a central valley and the surrounding mountains. The plain or the valley is approximately 2238 sq. km. accounting to 10% of the total state area. Out of this an area of 550 sq. km. is occupied by lakes, wetlands, barren uplands and hillocks. The valley is oval shape with a NNW-SSE orientation and has a gentle slope towards the south measuring 798 m above m.s.l. at the extreme north and 746 m above m.s.l. at the Southern end. The Imphal city stands at an altitude of 790 m above m.s.l.

GEOLOGY

Dayal and Duara (1963) outlined the classification of rocks in Manipur which is more or less in line with that of Oldham (1883) with some modifications after the views of Pascoe (1929) and Evans (1932). The geologic succession according to them is

Age	*Rock Type*
Recent to sub-recent	Alluvium
Oligocene	Barails
Intrusive rocks	Disang Series
Intrusive rocks (Cretaceous to early Eocene)	Surpentinities
Cretaceous	Axials

SEISMOLOGY

The hills of the whole zone of the eastern frontier of India including Manipur were built up during the late Pleistocene period and hence isostatic and seismic balances are yet to be attained. Manipur falls in one of the most seismically active zones of the Trans-Asiatic Earthquake Belt.

CLIMATE

Besides the influence by its locations around the latitudes just north of the Tropic of Cancer, the climate of the state is governed by the relief of land and the rain bearing winds viz. the South-West Monsoon in summer and the North-East Monsoon and the Mediterranean winds in winter. The eastern lowlands along the Indo-Burma border and the Western Assam Manipur border lowlands fall between the altitudes 30-100 metre above m.s.l. and thus reigned by a tropical climate. The Manipur Valley at a height of 780-800 metre above m.s.l. has sub-tropical climate while the higher reaches of the mountains surrounding the valley have a temperate climate.

RIVERS

Rivers along with other natural and man-made sources play an important role in irrigation in the state of Manipur. Irang, Barrak and Turel Achouba are some of the major rivers of the state.

Thoubal River : Thoubal river starts from Huimi hills of Ukhrul and flow westwards upto Yaingangpokpi and turning southwards, joins the Imphal river at Irong Ichin.

Iril River : It rises in the Lamkui and Kadam Hills of the north-eastern Mao. After flowing southwards, it joins the Imphal Rivers at Lilong area.

Barrak River : It is the biggest river of Manipur. Its source is 16 km east of Mao Police Station in Senapati District. Barrak, at its source is known as 'Sanglook'. It leaves Manipur area near Lalpur and flows towards Cachar, Assam. The Makru and the Irang are two main tributaries of this river.

Turel Achouba : Turel Achouba is also known as Imphal or Manipur river. It is the longest river of the state. Its source is Bolen Pat at 197 feet above sea level and 15 km from Kangpokpi area. It also joins the stream of Ningthee or Chindwin river of Burma in its way.

RIVERS IN HILL AREAS

Some of the important rivers of the hill areas of Manipur includes Makru, Barrak, Irang, Leimatak, Tuyungbi, Maklang, Chingai, Chalou, Taret Lok, Lokchao, Chakpi, Khuga and Tuivai river.

MAIN RIVERS : AT A GLANCE

River	Length (km.)	Aspect	Source	Destination
Barrak	84.39	West	Karong-Mao area	Brahmaputra River
Imphal	38	South	Bolen Pat in Kangpokpi area	Chindwin River
Iril	57.27	South	Lakhamai of Pural Block	Imphal River
Irang	28.13	South Western Block	Langka Chongjan area of Kangpokpi	Barrak River
Ithai	24.83	South	Selsi Thoubung area	Iril River

LAKES

The state of Manipur is characterised by numerous lakes. Many of them are also known for its scenic and aesthetic beauty. Loktak lake, the biggest of North East India, is also a part of Manipur. It is also famous for its great beauty.

LAKES IN HILL AREAS

There are two major lakes in hilly areas of Manipur. These are Kachouphung Lake in Ukhrul district and Zailad Lake in Tamenglong district.

MAIN LAKES : AT A GLANCE

Lakes	*District*	*Lakes*	*District*
❖ Loktak Lake	Bishnupur	❖ Kharung Pat	Bishnupur
❖ Heingang Pat	Imphal East	❖ Kachouphung Lake	Ukhrul
❖ Waithou Pat	Thoubal	❖ Pumlen Pat	Thoubal
❖ Utra Pat	Bishnupur	❖ Zailad Lake	Tamenglong
❖ Loushi Pat	Bishnupur	❖ Ikop Pat	Thoubal
❖ Ishok Pat	Bishnupur	❖ Sana Pat	Bishnupur
❖ Loukoi Pat	Bishnupur		

HILLS

❖ Cheirao-Ching	❖ Chakka Nungba	❖ Somrah
❖ Chinganguba	❖ Kanpum	❖ Kasom
❖ Mayangkhang	❖ Kopru-Laimatol	❖ Nupitel
❖ Nunjaibong	❖ Khhunho Spurs	❖ Hawbi
❖ Yomadoung	❖ Thumion	❖ Koubru Leikha
❖ Bharuni	❖ Laison	❖ Thangjing
❖ Kala Naga	❖ Sirohi Frar	

WATERFALLS

Waterfalls		*District*
❖ Barrak Waterfalls	:	Tamenglong
❖ Sadu Chiru Waterfalls	:	Bishnupur
❖ Khayang Waterfalls	:	Ukhrul
❖ Leimram Waterfalls	:	Bishnupur
❖ Dilily Waterfalls	:	Ukhrul

CAVES

Caves	*District*	*Caves*	*District*
❖ Tonglon	Churachandpur	❖ Sangboo	Chandel
❖ Tharon	Tamenglong	❖ Khangkhui	Ukhrul
❖ Hungdung Mangva	Ukhrul	❖ Khukse	Churachandpur

PEAKS

Peaks	*Height (m)*	*District*
❖ Leikot	2,832	Tamenglong
❖ Tampaba	2,564	—
❖ Mount Tenipu (Essau)	2,994	Senapati
❖ Siroi	2,835	Ukhrul
❖ Khayangbung	2,833	Ukhrul

THE PEOPLE

There is not much of historical evidence available on the origin of the people of Manipur. There are different schools of thought regarding the origin.

The people of Manipur are simple and largely untouched by the pollution of modern living. Their wants are few, they love outdoor life, find communion with nature and depend on the gifts of nature like rice for food, fish to supplement their dish.

MEITEIS

The Meiteis are mainly populating the main valley. Men are muscular and stout with well developed chest and hard limbs. They possess enormous stamina and muscular power. The dress of a man is white kurta, dhoti and pagari (old man).

Their houses are well adapted to the climatic conditions. The rich construct houses on the posts and beams with wood, and the poor with Bamboo. The common profession among men is agriculture. The educated folk seek official jobs and some engage themselves in different kinds of business. Fish is the common article of diet. Meiteis do not take meat and purely vegetarians but fish is not considered non-vegetarian.

KUKIS

The Kukis are also called Khongjois. They are distributed widely in Manipur, occupying the south-western, south and south-eastern hills which spread in the district of Churachandpur, Tangnoupal district and Sadar hills in the north Manipur. Kukis are of Mongoloid stock. The Men are short as well as medium sized. Their face is broad and round. The cheek-bones prominently bulged with bulged eye-sockets.

The houses of Kukis are raised above the ground. The floor is made of split bamboo and if wood is available, then of wooden planks. The men generally wear a cloth round the waist and cover the body above with a coarse sheet. A ceremonial dress is more colourful. The chief is the owner of the land and the forest of a certain area in that locality. Rice is the staple food. They have certain restrictions in eating animal flesh. The intoxicating drink is rice beer, both men and women enjoy it. It is served to the guests on all ceremonial occasions. Smoking is common among the men and women.

NAGA TRIBES

The Nagas occupy the northern, north-eastern, and north-western hills of Manipur. The different groups of Nagas are Thangkhuls, Mao, Muram Nagas, Tadubi, Kolya, Khoiras or Mayang Khong, Kabuis, Koirengs, Chirus and Marings. Nagas are of Mongoloid stock. The skin colour varies according to the habitat. The Tangkhuls, Mao-Muran Nagas are generally fairer as compared to the Kabus. The men are muscular and sturdy and full of stamina.

The dress is of simple form. In the case of men it is a piece of cloth wrapped round the waist, its ends are allowed to hang down. Nagas are expert and bow fight, spear throwing and in the use of Dao. All tribes keep Dao. The Naga village is always situated on a ridge in the hills especially at a convenient place where water is in the land or near by. Their houses are constructed on wooden poles. Rice is the staple food.

LOIS

The Lois consider themselves as the oldest inhabitants. Lois means 'slaves or dependent'. These small tribals inhabit the valley of Manipur. They are called Singmei, Undro and Chairel. All of them speak different dialects but with a considerable mixture of Manipuri words.

Physical Features : Lois are of Mongoloid stock but feature-wise, with sharp features, resemble the Aryans.

The Lois are expert at agriculture and hold monopoly in the silk, iron smelting and other craft work. Now they have been given scheduled caste status and the state government is taking interest in their uplift.

MUSLIMS

Muslims are living in several villages at Mayang, Imphal, Yaripok, Lylong, Thoubal etc. Their main occupation is agriculture. Some educated ones also seek official jobs in state and central government service. They are intelligent and hard-working persons. They have mixed characters of Mongoloid and Aryans in their features. They follows all norms of the Muslim society.

SIKHS

The Sikhs settled in Manipur are of Punjab origin but most of them have come from Burma where they had gone from Punjab in earlier times. Some of them entered Manipur after the Second World War and some others after the Burmese government disallowed them the citizenship. They have Gurudwaras at Imphal and Moreh. All Sikhs are businessmen dealing in transport, cloths and contracts etc. They are pioneer transporters in Manipur.

NEPALIS

The Nepalis are the old settlers in Manipur. The contribution of Nepalis to the Manipuri society is valuable. Most of the Nepalis entered Manipur as servants and labourers and settled here. Some started cultivation of the tribal chief's land as tenants with sufficient share of the crops. They were known for cattle rearing. Most of the settlers started dairies along with their agriculture. Nepalis have scattered into small valleys in Mao, Maram, Karong and Kangpokpi areas.

BISHNUPURIS

Some people of lower caste entered Manipur and they got good promises for their labour and jobs. Safaiwalas, cobblers, watermen, gardeners, washermen etc. were not available. Manipur being a casteless society was unmindful of these requirements. In Manipur these jobs are done by all. There are some Sudra Manipuris who are supposed to be the descendants of immigrants who married Manipuri women. This is also a degraded class called Kalacheiya or Bishnupuris which consists of descendants of Doms and other Bengalis of low castes. They have played an important role in the society. In Manipuri society they are respected. There is no concept of untouchability. Those who are declared bonafide citizens of Manipur get the reservation benefits.

BIHARIS

Most of the labour class comprises people of Bihar and Uttar Pradesh. They have come here to earn their bread. They are fluent in Meitei as well as in Tribal dialects. They have established themselves throughout the valley on all routes.

PUNJABIS

There are some non-Sikh Punjabi traders settled at Imphal. Their contribution to Punjabi culture is worth mentioning. Their dishes are very tasty. They retain their habit of speaking Punjabi amongst themselves. They speak in a hilarious and jubilant mood. Their women wear salwar-kurta, sari and are very fond of cosmetics. Inside Punjabi house one finds several items of furniture and comfort. They believe in decent living and eating.

MARWARIS

Marwaris are the dominating business community in the north-eastern region. They deal in big business and wholesale trade. Their concentrations are only in the established old towns and business centres like Imphal, Churachandpur and Moreh. They have entered Manipur in the late nineteenth and early twentieth century.

SOUTH INDIANS

Moreh town of Manipur is the real settlement of Tamils and Keralites. Most of them are refugees from Burma. They have introduced Idli and Dosa, the famous snack dishes of South Indians to the Meiteis and tribals. The men dress is lungi and shirt. Office goers wear pants and shirts. The women wear sari and blouse. They are all Hindus and a few Christians may also be there. Moreh Tamils are all Hindus and have established several temples of Kali, Durga and Shiva in the town. They also celebrate their festivals with great pomp and show.

BENGALIS

The Bengalis are the old settlers in Manipur. Due to the geographical closeness with Bengal the land has experienced a lot in respect of socio-cultural and socio-religious interaction between the two societies. The contribution of Bengalis to the Manipuri society is valuable. Bengalis are one of the most advanced and intellectually superb ethnical group of India.

GOVT. RECOGNISED TRIBES

The Government of Manipur has recognised 32 tribes in the state. These are as follows:

1. Aimol	9. Anal	17. Angami	25. Chiru
2. Chothe	10. Gangte	18. Hmar	26. Kabui
3. Kacha Naga	11. Kharam	19. Koirao	27. Koireng
4. Kom	12. Lamgang	20. Lusai Tribes	28. Maram
5. Maring	13. Mao	21. Monsang	29. Mayon
6. Paite	14. Poumi Naga	22. Purum	30. Ralte
7. Sema	15. Simte	23. Sahlte	31. Tangkhul
8. Tarao	16. Thadou	24. Vaiphei	32. Zou

ART AND CULTURE

FOLK DANCES

Some Famous folk dances of Manipur are as follows:

Ras Lila : The Ras Lila, the epitome of Manipuri classical dance is inter-woven through the celestial and eternal love of Radha and Krishna as has been described in the Hindu scriptures and reveals the sublime and transcendental love of Krishna and Radha and the Gopies' devotion to the Lord. It is generally performed in an enclosure in front of the temple throughout the night and watched with a deep sense of devotion. Ras performances are seasonal and varied and performed at the temple of Shree Shree Govindajee in Imphal on the nights of Basanta Purnima, Sarada Purnima and Kartik Purnima and at local temples later. Ras performances are mainly of four types—Vasanta Ras, Kunja Ras, Maha Ras and Nata/Nitya Ras. At the temple of Shri Shri Govinda, Vasanta Ras is performed on the full-moon night of Hiyangei (November). After they are performed at the temple of Shri Shri Govinda, they are performed at any time of the year.

Nupa Pala : Nupa Pala which is otherwise known as Kartal Cholom or Cymbal Dance is a characteristic of the Manipuri style of dance and music. The initial movements of this dance are soft and serene, gradually gathering momentum. It is a group performance of male partners, using cymbals and wearing snow white ball-shaped large turbans, who sing and dance to the accompaniment of Mridanga, an ancient classical drum "Pung" as it is called in Manipuri. The Nupa Pala acts as a prologue to the Ras Lila dances, besides an independent performance too, in connection with religious rites.

Pung Cholom : Pung or Manipuri Mridanga is the soul of Manipuri Sankirtana music and Classical Manipuri Dance. Khuyoi Tompok who ruled over Manipur during (154-264 A.D) introduced the pung having only one beating face. Since then, it has developed to the present form of 'Meitei Pung with two beating faces. Today, 'Pung Cholom' which is a traditional dance form of the pung drummers has earned international acclamation for its charming artistic display.

Maibi Dance : During the festival of Lai-Haraoba which is an annual ritual festival of the Meiteis, the inhabitants of the valley of Manipur, the Maibis, the priestesses considered to be spritural mediums, trace through their dances the whole concept of cosmogony of the Meitei people and describe their way of life. Beginning with the process of creation, they show the construction of houses and various occupations of the people to sustain themselves. It is a kind of re-living of the way of life of the past.

Khamba Thoibi Dance : Khamba Thoibi dance is a duet of male and female partners, a dance of dedication to the sylvan deity, Thangjing of Moirang, is the depiction of the dance performed by Khamba and Thoibi, the hero and heroine of the Moirang episode of the hoary past. This, with the "Maibi" dance (Priestess dance), the "Leima Jagoi" etc. form the "Lai Haraoba" dance. The "Lai Haraoba" dance, in many ways, is the fountainhead of the modern Manipuri dance form. This dance is a part and parcel of Moirang Lai-Haraoba. It is believed that the legendary hero - Khamba, and heroin - Thoibi danced together before the Lord Thangjing, a celebrated deity of Moirang, a village in the South-West of Manipur which is known for its rich cultural traditions, for peace and prosperity of the land.

SOME IMPORTANT TRIBAL DANCES OF MANIPUR

1. Kabui Naga Dance
2. Tangkhul Naga Dance – *Tangkhul Hunting Dance, Tangkhul War Dance, Lakhahganui Dance i.e., Virgin Dance etc.*
3. Tarao War Dance etc.
4. Mao Maram Dance
5. Paite Dance – *Dak Lam, Jangta Lam, Phit Lam, Ton Lam and Silam Lam*
6. Thadou Kuki Dance

FOLK SONGS

Some famous folk songs of Manipur are as follows:

Wari Liba : It is an indigenous art form of telling stories prevalent in the State since the 17th century. The Mahabharata and the Ramayana are the themes of such story telling.

Khulang Ishei : Manipuri folk song is known as 'Khulang Ishei'. It is popular for its thematic and romantic contents. The folk songs are commonly sung by the rural folk and hill men at the time of harvesting, collecting firewood, hunting and fishing.

Khongjom Parva : It is a musical narration of the Battle of Khongjom fought between the Manipuris and the British in April 1891. Dhobi Leinou started singing Khongjom Parva by thumping his hands on the knee and some times used an empty tin to thump upon. The Khongjom

Parva narrators glorify the Manipuris soldiers who sacrificed their lives for the sake of their motherland. Today the theme of singing Khongjom Parva includes the stories of Khamba and Thoibi, the Ramayana, the Mahabharata and the exploits of the kings of Manipur. The singer uses only a Dholak while singing.

Pena-Ishei : It is an ancient folk song of Manipur which is sung with a musical instrument called "Pena". This song narrates the popular stories of Manipur. Pena is a stringed musical instrument of Manipur. Its origin may be traced back to a hoary past. It is called Bena in parts of Assam. It is made up of two parts viz the penamasa and pena cheijing. Earlier, Pena was usually played by its player to invoke the gods and goddesses. But today, this musical instrument is played in musical concerts and other performances also.

Ougri : This is a very ancient type of song and sung usually in praise of Sun, Moon, Kings etc. It is mostly sung in Lai Haraoba festivals.

Moibung Esei : The conch music of Manipuri is quite distinct and extraordinary. An artist of it can blow two conches simultaneously producing enchanting music.

Nat Esei : It is a peculiar type of song composed and originated by the Manipuris. It is sung in both Manipuri and Bengali languages and the theme is usually of Hindu Gods and Goddesses.

Khubak Esei : This kind of song is performed by two sides of participants standing at opposite sides and facing at each other. The rhythmic clapping of palms is its accompanying music.

Khulang Esei : This kind of song is sung without any musical instrument and the theme of this type of song is related to love & romance. It is known as Heplee in archaic language.

TRADITIONAL MUSICAL INSTRUMENTS

1. Pung (Drum)
2. Kartal (Cymbals)
3. Pena (Sitar)
4. Manjira or Mandilla (Metal jingles)
5. Sipa (Flute)
6. Tingteila (Violin)
7. Mazo (Women's mouth-piece)
8. Khol (Drum), etc.

DANCE & CULTURE TRAINING INSTITUTES

- Government Dance College (Shree Shree Govindajee Natanalya) – Palace Compound, Imphal.
- J.N. Manipur Dance Academy – Near D.M. College Compound, Imphal.

MANIPURI STATE KALA AKADEMI

This Akademi was set up by the Government of Manipur in the year 1971. It is the first of its kind in the eastern region of India. It is an autonomous organization for the promotion and coordinating of cultural activities of the people of Manipur both of the valley and hills.

MUSEUM

MANIPUR STATE MUSEUM

This museum, located near the Imphal Pologround has a fairly good display of the state's heritage and a collection of portraits of Manipur's former rulers. Items of special interests are costumes, arms and weapons, relics and historical documents.

The Manipur State Museum was inaugurated by the late Prime Minister of India, Smt. Indira Gandhi on 23rd September, 1969. During 49 years, this Museum has become a fullfledged multipurpose Museum comprising of various Galleries like—Ethnology, Archeology, Natural History, Painting, Jallan, Children's Gallery and an open air gallery for housing the 78ft long boat called Hiyang Hiren (Royal boat).

Apart from the normal functions of Museum, it took up various activities like Museum awareness programmes, Conservation of Biological specimens, Cultural appreciation course, Science fairs, Thematic exhibition, Mobile exhibition etc.

Manipur State Museum has also taken up numerous sponsor programmes through National and International Museums.

IMPORTANT PLACES OF WORSHIP

All the communities and religions celebrate their respective religious festivals or days with devotion and unflinching commitment. Some of the major worship places are given below:

Kangla Temple	—	4th Assam Rifles Ground
Sanamahee Temple	—	1st Batalion, M.R.
Jain Digamber Temple	—	Paona Road
Govindajee Temple	—	Palace Ground
ISKON Temple	—	Airport Road
Hanuman Thakur Temple	—	Near Palace Ground
Gurdwar Temple	—	Thangal Bazar
Jame Masjid	—	Masjid Road
Hiyangthang Lairembi Temple	—	Hiyangthan
M.B.C. Central Church	—	Deulahland
Moirang Thangjing Temple	—	Moirang

FESTIVALS

Manipur celebrates a number of peculiar festivals of its own with great pomp and joy. Some of them are:

Lai-Haraoba : Lai Haraoba is one of the most important indigenous ritual festivals celebrated by the Meitei community of Manipur. It is celebrated to propitiate and please the ancestral deities to get their blessings in return. It depicts the act of creating universe and its objects, and unveils the endless journey of universe through its ritualistic performances. It is celebrated in Manipur since time immemorial and is being continued till today.

Yaoshang (Dol Jatra) : Celebrated for five days commencing from the full-moon day of Phalgun (February/March), Yaoshang is the premier festival of Manipur. The Thabal Chongba, a kind of Manipuri folk dance in which boys and girls hold hands and dance away their blues in festive tube-lit ambience is an inseparable part of the festival.

Ratha Jatra : One of the greatest festivals of the Hindus of Manipur, the festival is celebrated for about 10 days in the month of Ingen (June/July). Lord Jagannath leaves his temple in a Rath locally known as Kang pulled by pilgrims who vie with one another for this honour.

Ramjan ID (The premier festival of Manipur Muslims) : Ramjan Id is the most popular festival of the Manipuri Muslims (Meitei Pangal) and is observed in the usual spirits of joy and festivities as in other Muslim world. Ramjan is the ninth month of Hijri year.

Kut (Festival of Kuki-Chin-Mizo) : It is an autumn festival of the different tribes of Kuki-Chin-Mizo groups of Manipur. The festival has been variously described at different places amongst different tribes as Chavang-Kut or Khodou etc. It is a happy occasion for the villagers whose food stock is bountiful after a year of hard labour. The festival is a thanks giving feasts with songs and dances in merriment and joviality for all, in honour of the giver of an abundant harvest, it is observed on the first day of November every year.

Gang-Ngai (Festival of Kabui Nagas) : Celebrated for five days in the month of Wakching (December/January), Gang-Ngai is an important festival of the Kabui Nagas. The festival opens with the omen taking ceremony on the first day and the rest of the days are associated with common feast, dances of old men and women and of boys and girls, presentation of farewell gifts etc. From 1997, it starts from January 21.

Chumpha (Festival of Tangkhul Nagas) : Chumpha, generally the festival of Tangkhul Nagas, is celebrated for seven days in the month of December. It is a great festival of Tangkhul Nagas. The festival is held after harvest. The last three days are devoted to social gatherings and rejoicing. Unlike other festivals women play a special role in the festival. The concluding part of the festival ends with a procession within the village.

Christmas (Festival of Christians) : The Christmas is the greatest festival of all the Christians of Manipur, observed for two days on December 24 and 25. Prayers, reading of Gospels, eating, singing of hymns, lectures on Christ, sports etc., form the major part of the festival. In some villages where the inhabitants are well-off, the celebration continues till January 1 on which the New Years day is also observed.

Cheiraoba (The Manipur NewYear) : During the festival, people clean and decorate their houses and prepare special festive dishes which are first offered to various deities. Celebrated during the month of April, a part of the ritual entails villagers climbing the nearest hill tops in belief that it will enable them to rise to greater heights in their worldly life. The Pangals (Manipuri Muslims) also observe it

Heikru Hidongba : Celebrated in the month of September, a festival of joy, with little religious significance along a 16 metre wide boat. Long narrow boats are used to accommodate a large number of rowers. Idol of Lord Vishnu is installed before the commencement of the race.

Ningol Chakouba : It is a remarkable social festival of the Meiteis. Married women of the family who were married to distant places come to the parental house along with her children and enjoy sumptuous feast. It is a form of family rejoinder to revive familial affection. The festival is also observed by the Pangals to a certain extent now-a-days. It is observed on the second day of the new moon in the Manipuri month of Hiyangei (November).

Lui-Ngai-Ni : It is a collective festival of the Nagas observed on the 15th day of February every year. This is a seed-sowing festival after which tribes belonging to the Naga group begin their cultivation. Social gathering, songs, dances and rejoicing highlight the festivity. The annual festival also plays a great role in boosting the morale and strengthening the bond of Naga solidarity.

Kwak Jatra : Goddess Durga is propitiated with pomp and ceremony in this festival. It is celebrated in the month of October and represents the victory of righteousness over evil.

FESTIVALS OF MANIPUR : AT A GLANCE

Festivals	Celebrated by	Time of Celebration
❍ Lai Haraoba	Meiteis	May
❍ Rath Yatra	Hindus	July
❍ Yaoshang (Dol Jatra)	Hindus	February/March
❍ Christmas	Christians	25th December
❍ Mahavir Jayanti	Jains	April
❍ Depawali	Hindus	October / November
❍ Cheiraoba	Meiteis	April
❍ Chumpha	Tangkhul Nagas	December
❍ Gan Ngai	Kabui Nagas	16th January
❍ Heikru Hitongba	Meiteis	September
❍ Kwak Yatra (Durga Puja)	Hindus	September / October
❍ Kut	Kuki Chin Mizos	November
❍ Lui-Ngai-Ni	Nagas	15th February
❍ Mera Nongma Panba	Meiteis	September
❍ Ningol Chakkouba	Meiteis	November

SOME TRIBAL FESTIVALS OF MANIPUR

Tribes	*Festivals*
Anal	Sungkhomlkham, Mikhemphan, lkam, Philthabla, Inhla, etc.
Aimol	Reeyan
Chothe	Inampeilin
Hmar	Butu Chonglawa
Kabui	Gan-Ngai
Kharam	Lamtoul Kalouh
Kuki	Chapchar Kut, Mimkut, Chavang Kut
Mao	Chithuni
Naga	Lui-Ngai-Ni
Tangkhul	Shimsak Kasa, Chumpha, Thisham, Yarra, Mangkhap, Luira, Darreo etc.
Thadou	Chon
Zeliangrong	Gudui Ngai, Rih Ngai

EDUCATION

Education is an important aspect to demand one's right and thus it is essential for all. It is a key to making women self-reliance and giving them the confidence to pursue their goals and aspirations. The view in this context has been a life-long process and not a terminal point at the stage of people needed organic linkages between education and society. The Kothari Commission on education had stressed the need of such linkages in its report entitled 'Education and National Development'. UNESCO's goal of 'Education for All' had to be made aware to all sections of community and the people irrespective of caste and creed.

However, in India the Central Government in co-operation with State Governments continues to play a leading role in the evolution and monitoring of educational policies and programmes. This can be understand as the literacy rate of India in 1951 was 18.33% while in 2011 it was 73.0%. The same is the case with state of Manipur as literacy rate of state in 2011 was 76.94% as compared to 11.4% of 1951.

TRENDS OF LITERACY IN MANIPUR

Women in Manipur started receiving education since 1899. But the percentage of literacy rate of women was than very low. However, with the changing of times, it has been increased rapidly. It has shown improvement from 2.36% in 1951 to 70.26% in 2011. Male literacy trends too, have shown improvements from 20.77% in 1951 to 83.58% in 2011. The improvements in female literacy rates have been faster. Table 1 and Table 2 show the literacy rate of male and female and the district wise literates and population and literacy rate in Manipur.

Table 1: Literacy Rate in the State since 1951

Year	*Total Population*	*Total P.C*	*Male*	*Female*
1951	5,77,635	11.4	20.77	2.36
1961	7,80,037	30.4	45.12	15.93
1971	10,72,753	32.9	46.40	19.53
1981	14,20,953	41.3	53.29	29.06
1991	18,37,149	59.9	71.63	47.60
2001	2,388,634	68.87	77.87	59.70
2011	2,855,794	76.94	83.58	70.26

Source: Census of India 2011.

Table 2: District Wise Literates Number and Literacy Rate in Manipur, 2011 Census

District	*No. of Literates*			*Literacy Rate#*		
	Person	**Male**	**Female**	**Person**	**Male**	**Female**
Senapati	2,64,477	1,48,012	1,16,465	63.60	69.21	57.67
Tamenglong	85,006	47,403	37,603	70.05	76.09	63.69
Churachandpur	1,95,935	1,04,013	91,922	82.78	86.97	78.50
Chandel	90,302	51,053	39,249	71.11	77.78	63.96
Ukhrul	1,29,829	70,148	59,631	81.35	85.52	76.95
Imphal (E)	3,24,664	1,73,314	1,51,350	81.95	88.77	75.32
Imphal (W)	3,92,626	2,05,985	1,86,641	86.08	92.24	80.17
Bishnupur	1,56,333	87,313	69,020	75.85	85.11	66.68
Thoubal	2,69,304	1,52,617	1,16,687	74.47	85.00	64.09
Manipur	**1,908,476**	**1,039,858**	**8,68,568**	**76.94**	**83.58**	**70.26**

Note: #*Literacy rate is the percentage of literates to total population aged 7 years and above.*

In 2011, the district wise rate of female literacy was highest in Imphal West. Churachandpur registers second highest rate with 78.5%. The lowest rate of female literacy was in Senapati district being 57.6% only.

NUMBER OF INSTITUTIONS IN MANIPUR

Year	Number of Institutions							All Institutions
	University	College for			School for			
		General Education	Professional education	Total	General Education	Professional & other education	Total	
1950-51	–	1	–	1	537	–	537	538
1960-61	–	2	1	3	2029	314	2343	2346
1970-71	–	12	14	26	2979	389*	3369	3394
1980-81	–	24	41	65	3576	511	4087	4152
1990-91	1	29	33	62	4307	2,492	6799	6862
2000-01	2	61	13	74	3970	78*	4048	4124

* *Due to cancellation of non-formal education*

Year	Number of Institutions							All Institutions
	University	College for			School for			
		General Education	Professional education	Total	General Education	Professional & other education	Total	
2010-11	–	–	–	–	4358	–	4358	4358**
2011-12	–	–	–	–	4458	–	4458	4458**
2012-13	–	–	–	–	4579	–	4579	4579**
2013-14	–	–	–	–	4696	–	4696	4696**
2014-15	–	–	–	–	4403	–	4403	4403**
2015-16	–	–	–	–	3676	–	3676	3676**

** *Excluding Colleges and University*

UNIVERSITIES IN MANIPUR

MANIPUR UNIVERSITY

Establishment : June 5, 1980, under the Manipur University Act, 1980 (Manipur Act No.VIII of 1980).

Location : Canchipur

The University has the following three Schools of Studies consisting of 22 Post-Graduate Departments including the Manipur Institute of Management studies.

- School of Sciences
  Disciplines : Anthropology, Biochemistry, Chemistry, Computer Science, Earth Science, Geography, Life Sciences, Mathematics, Physics and Statistics
- School of Social Sciences
  Disciplines : Commerce, Economics, Education, History, Library & Information Science, Political Science and Management Studies
- School of Humanities
  Disciplines : English, Hindi, Linguistics, Manipuri and Philosophy

CENTRAL AGRICULTURE UNIVERSITY

Central Agricultural University
Iroisemba, Imphal - 795 004, Manipur (India)
Courses Offered :

- B.Sc. (Agri)
  (Four year duration)
- M.Sc. (Agri)
  (a) Agronomy (b) Plant Pathology

(c) Horticulture (d) Plant Breeding & Genetics
(e) Soil Science & Agril. Chemistry (f) Entomology

Department Under CAU

Agronomy, Horticulture, Botany & Plant Pathology, Plant Breeding & Genetics, Soil Science & Agril. Chemistry, Entomology, Agril. Economics, Extension Education, Agril. Enginneering, Animal Sciences, Math & Statistics and Language (English).

COLLEGES IN MANIPUR

AFFILIATED COLLEGE

Bishnupur District
1. Mangolnganbi College, Ningthoukhong
2. S. Kula Women's College, Nambol
3. Kumbi College, Kumbi

Thoubal District
✧ W. Mani Girls College, Thoubal

FACT FILE

- The Council of Higher Secondary Education, Manipur was established in 1992. The council is located at Babupura, Imphal.
- Manipur Board of Secondary Education was established in 1972-73.
- The Deaf & Mute School and the Government Ideal Blind School are in Takyel.
- Rastra Bhasa (Hindi) Promotion Centres are also working in Manipur. These are Manipur Hindi Parishad, Assembly Road; Manipur Rastra Bhasa Pachyar Samiti, Paona Bazar and Manipur Hindi Pachyar Sabha, Akampat.
- There are some Sanskrit Study Centres in Manipur as well. These are Rajyaka Sanskrit Toll (College) in D.M. College compound; Vishwanath Sanskrit Vidyalaya at Kakching and Manipur Sanskrit Mahavidyalaya at Brahmpur Nahabam.
- The present 10+2+3 system of education was started in Manipur from the academic session of 1986-87.
- The State Institute of Journalism was established on 19th October 1992.

SOME IMPORTANT DAYS OF MANIPUR

❖ ***Statehood Day :*** 21st January ❖ ***Sportspersons' Day:*** 25th February ❖ ***Khongjom Day :*** 23rd April ❖ ***Patroit's Day :*** 13th August ❖ ***Manipuri Language Day :*** 20th August ❖ ***Manipur Integrity Day :*** 28th September ❖ ***Irabot's Day:*** 30th September ❖ ***Nupee Lal Day :*** 12th December

JUDICIARY

MANIPUR HIGH COURT

Finally the long cherished dream of the people of Manipur, particularly the legal fraternity, has been fulfilled with the then Chief Justice of India Altamas Kabir inaugurated the Manipur High Court on March 25, 2013. Former Chief Justice of Chhattishgarh AM Sapre was sworn in as the first Chief Justice of Manipur High Court on March 23, 2013. Justice Sapre, was the first Chief Justice of the newly-set up Manipur High Court. The court would have three judges including Justice Sapre in the beginning. Judge of Guwahati High Court N. Koteswar had been appointed as a judge of Manipur High Court. The inaugural function held at the newly constructed High Court complex at Chingmeirong was attended by former Union Law Minister Dr. Ashwini Kumar, Chief Minister O. Ibobi, Gauhati High Court Chief Justice A.K. Goyal and two Supreme Court Judges. Manipur was within the jurisdiction of the Imphal Bench of Gauhati High Court till March 25, 2013. Earlier, the Imphal Bench of Gauhati High Court came into existence on 21st January 1972, the day Manipur attained its statehood.

SUBORDINATE JUDICIARY

The courts of Manipur are divided into two divisions, viz Manipur East and Manipur West. Manipur East comprises of Imphal East, Imphal West and Ukhrul whereas Manipur West comprises of Bishnupur, Thoubal, Churachandpur, Tamenglong, Senapati and Chandel. There are two District courts & two Session Courts in Manipur headed by one District and Sessions Judge each. A number of subordinate Courts at the District and subordinate level come under these District Courts.

DISTRICT COURT

The code of Civil Procedure, 1908 regulates procedures of conduct of cases by all Civil Courts and it came into force since 1st January, 1909. The District Court is subordinate to the High Court and every Civil Court of a grade inferior to that of a district Court and every Court of small causes is subordinate to the High Court and District Court. It is headed by a District Judge appointed by the Manipur High Court, Imphal. Other subordinate courts like Additional District Court, Senior Division and Junior Division are lower hierarchies next to the Manipur

High Court, Imphal. Each of these courts were established under different sections directed by Supreme Court which was passed by the Parliament from time to time.

CRIMINAL COURT

The code of Criminal Procedure 1973 has come into effect from April 1, 1974. The Courts for Criminal cases are established in accordance with the provisions of the code of Criminal Procedure 1974. The Criminal Procedure code is mainly an adjective law of procedure. The object of the code of Criminal Procedure is to provide a machinery for the punishment of offenders against the substantive Criminal law such as the Indian Penal code. The Sessions Court is the highest criminal court subordinate to the High Court and the subordinate Courts of the Chief Judicial Magistrate, the Additional Chief Judicial Magistrate and the Judicial Magistrate first class.

COMMISSION

Manipur Human Rights Commission, Lamphelpat was established on 27th June 1998 under the Protection of Human Rights Act, 1993. The main purpose is for protection of human rights and prevention of violation of human rights. A person can make a complaint for violation of human rights to the State Commission. The Commission at present consists of four members headed by one chairperson.

Courts of Manipur East

District	*Court Name*	*Location*
Imphal East	District & Sessions Court	Uripok Cheirap Court Complex, Imphal - 795001
Imphal East	Addl District & Sessions Court	Uripok Cheirap Court Complex, Imphal-795001
Imphal East	Civil Judge (Sr Division) No II Court	Lamphel Court Complex, Imphal - 795004
Imphal East	Chief Judicial Magistrate Court	Uripok Cheirap Court Complex, Imphal - 795001
Imphal East	Addl Chief Judicial Magistrate Court	Lamphel Court Complex, Imphal - 795004
Ukhrul	Chief Judicial Magistrate Court	Ukhrul
Ukhrul	Civil Judge (Jr Divn) Court	Ukhrul

Imphal East	Civil Judge (Jr Divn) Court	Lamphel Court Complex, Imphal - 795004
Jiribam	Civil Judge (Jr Divn) Court	Jiribam
Imphal East	Judicial Magistrate First Class / Transport Court	Lamphel Court Complex, Imphal - 795004
Imphal East	Gauhati High Court, Imphal Bench	North AOC, Imphal-795001
Imphal East	Gauhati High Court, Imphal Bench	Lamphel Court Complex, Imphal - 795004
Imphal East	Civil Judge (Jr Divn) Court	Imphal - 795001

Courts of Manipur West

District	*Court Name*	*Location*
Imphal West	Manipur West Court	Uripok Cheirap Court Complex, Imphal-795001
Imphal West	Manipur West Court	Uripok Cheirap Court Complex, Imphal-795001
Imphal West	Civil Judge Sr Division Court	Lamphel,Court Complex, Imphal-795004
Tamenglong	CJM, Tamenglong Court	Lamphel,Court Complex, Imphal-795004
Chandel	CJM, Chandel Court	Lamphel,Court Complex, Imphal-795004
Senapati	CJM, Senapati Court	Lamphel,Court Complex, Imphal-795004
Thoubal	CJM, Thoubal Court	Thoubal
Thoubal	Civil Judge Jr Division, Thoubal Court	Thoubal
Bishnupur	CJM, Bishnupur Court	Bishnupur
Bishnupur	Civil Judge Jr Division Judicial Court	
Churachandpur	CJM, Churachandpur	Churachandpur
Imphal West	Special Court (NDPS)	Lamphel,Court Complex, Imphal-795004
Imphal West	Family Court	Lamphel, Court Complex, Imphal-795004

Departments In Manipur

To implement various schemes, projects and plans following Departments and Boards/Corporations are functioning in the State of Manipur.

LIST OF DEPARTMENTS

S.No.	*Name of Department*	*S.No.*	*Name of Department*
1.	Adult Education	2.	Family Welfare
3.	Art and Culture	4.	Forest & Environment
5.	Agriculture	6.	Fishery
7.	Commerce and Industries	8.	Fire Service
9.	Controller of Technical Education	10.	Food and Civil supply
11.	Co-operation	12.	Gauhati High Court
13.	District Session Judge (east)	14.	Horticulture & Soil Conservation
15.	Education (S)	16.	Irrigation and Flood Control
17.	Electricity Department	18.	Information and Public Relations
19.	Economics & Statistics	20.	Institutional Finance Cell
21.	Election Department	22.	Jail (Prisons)
23.	Employment Exchange	24.	Labour
25.	Excise Department	26.	Local Fund Audit
27.	Family Court	28.	Lottery
29.	MAHUD	30.	Manipur Police Wireless
31.	Manipur Public Service Commission	32.	Minority and Backward Classes
33.	Medical and Health	34.	Public Work Department
35.	Public Health Engineering	36.	Planning
37.	Printing and Stationary	38.	Rural Development & Panchayati Raj
39.	Sericulture	40.	Settlement and Land Record
41.	State Academy of Training	42.	State Council of Educational Research and Training (SCERT)
43.	State Election Commission	44.	Taxation
45.	Tourism	46.	Town Planning
47.	Treasury and Accounts	48.	Tribal Development
49.	Veterinary and Animal Husbandry	50.	Transport
51.	Vigilance		

LIST OF BOARDS/CORPORATIONS/OTHERS

S.No.	Name of Department	S.No.	Name of Department
1.	Council of Higher Secondary Education, Babupara	2.	Manipur Industrial Dev. Corpn. Ltd.
3.	Imphal Municipal Council	4.	Manipur Police Housing Corpn. Ltd.
5.	J.N. Manipur Dance Academy	6.	Manipur State Co-operative Bank
7.	Manipur Food Industries Corporation Ltd.	8.	Manipur State Road Transport Corporation
9.	Loktak Development Authority	10.	Manipur State Social Welfare Advisory Board
11.	Manipur Aids Control Society	12.	Manipur Tribal Development Corporation
13.	Manipur Development Society (MDS)	14.	Planning and Development Authority, Manipur
15.	Manipur Handloom & Handicraft Corpn. Ltd		

Manipur Public Service Commission

Under Article 315(4) of the Constitution, the Union Public Service Commission (UPSC) agreed to function as the Public Service Commission of the State of Manipur till October 21, 1972.

On October 3, 1972 the Governor of Manipur issued the order of constitution of the Manipur Public Service Commission under Article 318 with one Chairman and two Members. Shri B.K. Nehru, Governor of Manipur inaugurated the office of the Manipur Public Service Commission at a glittering function on October 23, 1972 at the Gandhi Memorial Hall, Imphal. The then Chief Minister, Shri Alimuddin presided over the function.

Manipur Science & Technology Council

The Manipur Science and Technology Council (MASTEC), Imphal is an autonomous apex organisation of Department of Science and Technology, Government of Manipur. It is an advisory body for the state in the field of Science and Technology. The technical secretariat of the Council is supported jointly by the Department of Science and Technology, Government of India and the Government of Manipur. The Council was established in the year 1985 and got registered in 1996.

Compositions

- Chief Minister, Manipur -- *Chairman*
- Minister (Science & Technology), Manipur--*Vice Chairman*
- Secretary Science & Technology, Govt. of Manipur--*Member Secretary*

Minerals

Minerals provide a base for the rapid industrialization. It is imperative, therefore, that proper attention is paid to their development. The State Government has formulated a New Mineral Policy (NMP). It is to develop mineral-based industries by identifying lack of infrastructure, lack of investment and flow of credit from banks and exploration of local resources and manpower to achieve the industrial growth. With the objective of the strengthening organisational set up, streamlining of mineral administrative machineries, augmentation and intensification of mineral exploration, commencement of mining activities and participation in general water exploration and geo-physical investigations, it is proposed to provide sufficient fund during the Ninth Five Year Plan. To achieve the objectives phasing programme for exploration and investigation of minerals, collaborative efforts for strengthening of the Geology and Mining Division is initiated by creating Mining section. So far 58 per cent of the total area of Manipur has been covered by systematic geological mapping and 42 per cent still remains to be covered.

The Geological Survey of India (GSI) has undertaken systematic survey in the three districts of Manipur viz. Ukhrul, Churachandpur and Chandel and discovered considerable quantities of valuable mineral deposits like limestone, copper, lignite, nickel, chromite, asbestos, salt etc. Some of the important mineral resources are given below.

LIMESTONE

Limestone is an important material for manufacturing of cement. It is mainly available in different parts of Ukhrul District viz. Hundung, Mata, Khangoi, Sokpao, Lambui and Kasom. It is also available between 32/4 and 32/6 milestone on Imphal Moreh Road in Chandel District. Limestones are located at Lambui, Kasom, Paorei, Phungcham, Kazing Malung, Shokpau, Yongphu, Shingda, Marao, Singkap, Shangshak, Koshu, Nungou, Mawai, Songphel, Siraukhong, Cretland, Chingsou, Humine, Makan, of Ukhrul District. Only in Ukhrul District, the total inferred deposit of limestone has been estimated to 6.35 million tonnes and 5.76 million tonnes at Phungyar and Meiring respectively.

ASBESTOS

The veins and veinlets of antigorite and chrysotile asbestos have been found in the massive serpentine bearing rocks near Moreh, Nepali Basti and Kwatha but none of these occurrences seem to be of economic importance. A small quantity of asbestos is also available in the eastern part of Ukhrul District.

CHROMITE

Deposits of chromite containing metallurgical grade have been located near the Shiroi hill of the Ukhrul District and hinted the possibility of large deposits in future. Besides, quantity of chromite is also available near the Nepali Basti of Chandel District covering an area of about 90 sq. km. and having maximum thickness of 0.3 metre.

More than 25 occurrences of chromite have so far been located in Manipur. These are located at Lunghar, Phangrai, Sirohi, Gamnom, Pushing, Khangkhui, Yentem, Nungbi, Hangkau, Apong, Chingai, Poi, Pinghang, Nampisha, Kangpat, and Chattrick Khunou of Ukhrul District and Kwatha, Sibong, Khudengthabi and Minou-Mangkang of Chandel District.

COPPER

The Geological Survey of India (GSI) has found copper in the Chandel District and Nickel containing copper sulphate, chalcopyrite, chalcocite and metals at Nungau and Kongal Thana. A small quantity of copper is also available at Ningthi & Kwatha of the Chandel District and Humie of the Ukhrul District.

NICKEL

Nickel associated with the serpentinite rock has been located at Nampesh and Kwatha areas of the Chandel District. The GSI in their geochemical and other methods has found metallic nickel dispersed in the soil in fairy high concentration of nickel varying upto 0.9 per cent. Soil samples in the Moreh area containing weathered serpentinite rock also show the availability of nickel varying from 0.24 to 0.9 per cent.

LIGNITE

The GSI has found deposits of lignite in Kangvai village of Turenloo valley of Churachandpur District. The total quantity of lignite has been estimated at 12,262 tonnes which can be used in manufacturing cement in the cement plant in Ukhrul district.

SALT

Salt is mainly available in Waikhong, Sikhong, Chandrakhong and Keithel Manbi. Most of the salt springs are being tapped by driving one metre diameter lined wells for manufacture of salt in a small-scale.

MINERALS AND THEIR PRODUCING AREAS

Sl.No.	*Mineral*	*Area*
1.	Limestone	Hundung, Phungyar, Meiring mata, Khangoi, Shokvao, Lambui & Kasom in Ukhrul
2.	Asbestos	Nepali basti, Kwatha, Moreh in Chandel
3.	Chromites	Vicinity of Shiroi hill, Ukhrul, Napali Basti in Chandel
4.	Coppers	Nigthi and Kwatha in Chandel, Humie in Ukhrul
5.	Nickel	Nambashi and Kwatha of Chandel
6.	Lignite	Kanvai village of Turenloo valley in Churachanpur
7.	Salt	Waikhong, Sikhong, Chandrakhong and Keithel Manbi.

Major Projects

The Department pursued with the Ministry of Mines, Government of India for obtaining clearance of a project proposal on mineral exploration namely "Contribution to a sustainable socio-economic development of Manipur State: Supply of equipment along with related assistance to Department of Geology & Mining, Government of Manipur" to be implemented with the assistance of BRGM, France. The proposal is under consideration of Ministry of Mines for onward transmission to the Ministry of Economic Affairs, Government of India. The estimated cost of the project is about ₹ 10.00 crore.

Another project proposal named "DOVEMAP" (Development of Village Economy through Mineral Appraisal Programme) has also submitted to the Ministry of Rural Development, Government of India for funding. The aim of the project is amongst other, to locate low cost but large potential mineral resources in the villages and to study various factors and parameters affecting development aspects of rural economy encompassing minerals, water and terrain for planned exploitation.

The Geology & Mining Division is also presently engaged in the sponsored works on geotechnical investigations of the Loktak Downstream Project, NHPC.

IRRIGATION AND POWER

Power or electricity is the most convenient and versatile form of energy. It plays a key role in the industrial, agricultural and commercial sectors of the economy and is also the most crucial source of supplying domestic energy requirements. The demand has, therefore, been growing at a rate faster than other forms of energy.

The power supply position in Manipur showed a marked improvement with the commissioning of the Loktak Hydro Electric Project in August, 1984. The demand of power was met mainly from Grid Power and a little from diesel and hydro generation. More emphasis was given to utilize Loktak Hydro Power to the maximum extent possible and to curtail the uneconomical generation of power from diesel generating sets.

The erstwhile Electricity Department, Manipur was unbundled and corporatized into the following two State Owned functionally independent successor entities w.e.f. 1st February, 2014, in pursuance of Electricity Act, 2003:

(I) Manipur State Power Company Limited (MSPCL)

(II) Manipur State Power Distribution Company Limited (MSPDCL)

Power Generation

The installed capacity of power in the state has remained the same as 11,845 KW during 1999-00 to 2001-02. However, during 2002-03 the installed capacity increased to 47,252 KW. During the year 2003-04 the installed capacity reduced to 47,052 KW. Then there was an increase from the years 2004-05 to the tune of 47,252 KW. The installed capacity were 45,020 KW, and 2.211 MW in 2011-12 and 2015-16 respectively.

REQUIREMENT OF POWER

The requirement of power for all categories of consumers viz., domestic, commercial, industrial, water works and public lighting has been gradually increasing year after another. This has been due to the fact that all the development activities like education, health care, telecommunication, electronic media and computerisation etc. have been depending by and large on electricity.

Demand and Supply of Power in Manipur

Year	*Power (MW)*		
	Demand	*Part of the Demand Met*	*Shortfall*
2010-11	184	110	74
2011-12	171	115	56
2012-13	201	119	82
2013-14	229	130	99
2014-15	262	232	30
2015-16	301	167.19	133.81

Source: Manipur State Power Distribution Company Limited, (MSPDCL).

AVAILABILITY OF POWER

The power supply in Manipur depends entirely on the share of power allocated from the Central sector plants namely, Loktak Hydro Electric Plant, Kopili-Khangdong Hydro Electric Plant, Assam Gas Based Power Plant at Kathalguri and Agartala Gas Turbine power plant at Ramchandranagar, Eastern Regional Electricity Board, Meghalaya State Electricity Board, Ranganadi Hydro Electric Plant and Doyang Hydro Electric Plant in the North Eastern region. The availability, however, decreases in the lean season when the generation is reduced following the recession of water levels in the rain fed reservoirs of the Central sector Hydel plants. Sometimes, the availability of the power from these plants was so poor that even the demand of vital installations like hospital, radio station, doordarshan kendra and other telecommunication stations could not be met. When the water levels in the Hydel plants went down below minimum draw down level, the generation is likely to be stopped anytime if rain does not come.

Share of Power from Central Sector, 2015-2016

Sl. No.	*Name of the Project*	*Installed Capacity MW*	*Share of Manipur*	
			Per cent	*MW*
1.	Loktak Hydro Electric Project (NHPC)	105	36.57	38.4*
2.	Khongdong HPS	50	5.33	3
3.	Kopilli + Kopilli HPS	200	6.17	12

Sl. No.	*Name of the Project*	*Installed Capacity MW*	*Share of Manipur*	
			Per cent	*MW*
4.	Kopilli HEP Stage-II	25	6.0	2
5.	Kathalguri GPS	291	6.9	23
6.	Agartala GPS	84	7.0	6
7.	Agartala GPS Extra Unit-I	23	6.85	1.6
8.	Doyang HPS	75	6.7	5
9.	Ranganadi HPS	405	7.16	29
10.	Pallatana GPP	726	5.79	42
	Total	1,984	94.47	162.00

**Inclusive of allocation of surrendered share 8 MW by Meghalaya to Manipur*
Source: Annual Administrative Report, 2015-16, Manipur State Power Company Limited

IRRIGATION

The state did not have any major and medium irrigation project up to 1972-73 and agriculture was solely dependent on capricious rainfall. Hence, assured water supply for irrigation is of utmost importance.

In fact, major, medium and multipurpose irrigation projects have been introduced very late in the state. Major and medium irrigation was started only from the 4th plan period onwards. The state has so far taken up 8 projects under the major, medium and multipurpose irrigation projects. Of these 8 projects, 3 projects namely Thoubal Project, Singda dam Project and Khuga dam Project are multipurpose. Loktak Lift Irrigation (LLI) is the major project and four are medium projects namely, Imphal Barage, Khoupum Dam, Sekmai Barrage and Dolaithabi projects. The Loktak Lift Irrigation Project is one of the biggest lift irrigation project in the North Eastern Region of India. Among these eight projects, three of them are on-going which are (i) Khuga Multipurpose Project, (ii) Thoubal Multipurpose Project & (iii) Dolaithabi Barrage Project. These 8 projects on completion will give an ultimate annual irrigation potential of 1,09,785 ha. with water supply and power components of 19 MGD and 10 MW respectively.

IMPORTANT PROJECTS IN MANIPUR

Project	*Company*	*Industry*
Thoubal Irrigation Project	Government of Manipur	Irrigation
Khuga Irrigation Project	Government of Manipur	Irrigation
Singda Irrigation Project	Government of Manipur	Irrigation
Dolaithabi Barrage Irrigation Project	Government of Manipur	Irrigation

WILDLIFE

At present, the protected area network of India comprises 104 national parks and 551 sanctuaries covering an area of 15.67 million hectares.

As far as the state of Manipur is concern, it has a special responsibility towards the rest of country and indeed the world at large. The mountains, foothills and plains house a zoogeographic diversity of flora and fauna. The species that are to be protected are, Sangai (dancing deer), Uchek Langmeidon (the great Indian hornbill), Nongyin etc.

NATIONAL PARKS AND WILDLIFE SANCTUARIES : AT A GLANCE

National Parks/ Wildlife Sanctuaries	Area Covered sq. km.	Location	Year of Decla- ration	Important Fauna
Sirohi National Park	41 sq. km.	Imphal East district	1982	Tiger, clouded leopard, leopard, jungle cat, wild dog, marten, serow, binturong, civets, sambar, barking deer, Himalayan black bear, etc.
Keibul Lamjao National Park	40 sq. km.	Imphal and Bishnupur district	1977	Sangai, leopard, cat, hog deer, fishing cat and a huge variety of water birds.
Bunning Wildlife Sanctuary	115.8 sq. km.	Tamenglong district	1997	Hoolock, gibbon, civet cat, hogbadger, stumped tail monkey, sambar, tragopan, etc.
Jiri Makru Wildlife Sanctuary	198 sq. km	Tamenglong district	1997	Slow loris, langur, yellow throated martin, hoolock gibbon, sambar, pied hornbill, leopard, great pied hornbill, etc.
Yaingoupokpi Lokchao Wildlife Sanctuary	184.80 sq. km.	Chandel district	1989	Tiger, leopard, hog deer, clouded, elephant, leopard and huge variety of bird etc.
Keilam Wildlife Sanctuary	187.5 sq. km.	Churachandpur district	1997	Hornbill, uchek langmeidon (the great Indian hornbill), tiger, leopard, elephant, etc.
Zeliad Wildlife Sanctuary	21 sq. km.	Tamenglong district	1997	Hog deer, bear, serow, tiger, wild dog, elephant, etc.

FOREST & ORCHIDS

For a hilly State like Manipur, forest products are the most important natural resources for environmental protection and maintaining ecological balance. According to Forest Report, 2017 by Forest Survey of India (FSI), Dehradun, the forest cover of Manipur is 17,346 sq. kms. as against 16,994 sq. kms. in 2015. The distribution of forest cover according to the FSI is shown in the Table below.

District-wise Forest Cover of Manipur (State of Forest Report 2017)

(Area in km²)

District	*Geographical Area*	*Very Dense Forest*	*Mod. Dense Forest*	*Open Forest*	*Total*	*Per cent of GA*
Bishnupur	496	0	1	21	22	4.44
Chandel	3,313	11	970	1,926	2,907	87.75
Churachandpur	4,570	42	1,663	2,464	4,169	91.23
Imphal East	709	0	61	217	278	39.21
Imphal West	519	0	16	38	54	10.40
Senapati	3,271	272	751	1,161	2,184	66.77
Tamenglong	4,391	390	1,754	1,809	3,953	90.03
Thoubal	514	0	2	71	73	14.20
Ukhrul	4,544	193	1,292	2,221	3,706	81.56
Grand Total	**22,327**	**908**	**6,510**	**9,928**	**17,346**	**77.69**

Forest plays threefold roles *i.e.*, protective, productive and aesthetic, each being equally important. Based on the legal status, the forest can be categorised as reserved, protected and unclassed forests. Reserved Forest is one which is permanently dedicated either to the production of timber or to other forest produces and in which right of grazing and cultivation is seldom allowed. In protected forests, these rights are allowed subject to a few mild restrictions. Unclassed Forest consists largely of inaccessible forest or unoccupied waste.

Area under Forest by Legal Status

Year	*Reserved Forests*	*Protected Forests*	*Unclassed Forests*	*Other Forests*	*Total*
2007-08	1,467	4,171	11,780	–	17,418
2008-09	1,467	4,171	11,780	–	17,418
2009-10	1,467	4,171	11,780	–	17,418
2010-11	1,467	4,171	11,780	–	17,418
2011-12	1,467	4,171	11,780	–	17,418
2012-13	1,467	4,171	11,780	–	17,418
2015-16	1,467	4,171	11,780	–	17,418
2016-17	1,467	4,171	11,780	–	17,418

CLASSIFICATION OF FORESTS

Area under forest includes all lands alassed as forests under any legal enactment dealing with forests or administered as forests whether state owned or private and whether wooded or maintained as potential forest land. The area of crops raised in the forests and grazing lands or area open for grazing within the forests are generally included under the forests area.

DIVISION OF FORESTS

In spite of its smallness in size, the state's vegetation is rich and varied in character. This is because of the different climatic conditions found in the state and its peculiar physiography. The forest area of the state falls into four distinct zones viz. (i) Burma Border Forests (ii) Ukhrul Pine Forests (iii) Forest overlooking the valley and (iv) Barak Drainage Forests. The Burma Border Forests lie along the Indo-Burma Border. The Kabaw Valley marks the eastern boundary of these forests. The Ukhrul pine forests are scattered almost all over the hills surrounding the valley area. The Barak Drainage forests area situated in the hills of the west of valley area along the cost of the Barak River and its tributaries viz. Jiri, Tuivai, Leimatak and Makru.

The main timber species available in Manipur are Teak, Uningthou, Khasi-pine, Dipterecarpes species (Yangou and Khangra), Michelia Champa (Leihao), Terminalia species (Tolhao), Cedrela Toona (Tairen), Schima Walliechii (Usoi) etc. The quality of timber available in Manipur is very suitable for furniture and construction purposes.

FOREST PRODUCTS

With a view to maintaining ecological balance, the Government has restricted the felling of trees in the forest areas. As a result, the felling of trees is done on limited scale. The production and value of forest products for 2015-16 is shown at Table below.

Outturn and Value of Forest Production of Manipur

(Value: ₹ in lakhs)

Sl. No.	Name of Product	Unit	2015-16	
			Quantity	Value
(1)	(2)	(3)	(4)	(5)
I.	Major Forest Product			
	1. Teak	Cum.	—	—
	2. Timber other than teak	Cum.	3190.637	81.31
	3. Fire wood	MT	35360.04	52.39
II.	Minor Forest Products			
	1. Cane	Rm.	90000	0.72
	2. Stone	Cum.	338507	133.85
	3. Sand	Cum.	750507	27.58
	4. Earth	Cum.	1286	1.44
	5. Thatching Grass	Bdls.	—	—
	6. Bamboo	Nos.	1658487	14.12
	7. Charcoal	Qtl.	861	1.47
	8. Broom	Kg.	523045	3.32
	9. Ginseng	Kg	5709.03	14.41
	10. Miscellaneous			40.12

Source: Forest Department, Government of Manipur.

ORCHIDS

Blessed with an amazing variety of flora and fauna, 67% of the geographical area of Manipur is hill tract covered forests. Depending on the altitude of hill ranges, the climatic condition varies from tropical to sub-alpine. The wet forests and the pine forests occur between 900-2700 m above MSL and they together sustain a host of rare and endemic plant and animal life. Coveted the world over as some of the most beautiful and precious blooms, orchids have an aura of exotic, mysteries about them.

In Manipur, they are abound in their natural habitat growing in soil or on trees and shrubs speaking their beauty and colour, stunning the eye that is not used to seeing them in such profusion. There are 500 varieties of orchids which grow in Manipur of which 472 have been identified.

TOURISM

Spread over an area of 22,327 sq. km., and a population of over 28.55 lakh (2011 census), Manipur is a State with a glorious history and rich and varied culture. The scenic beauty, large natural fresh water lake surrounded by hills, refreshing waterfalls and exotic orchids make Manipur a place of prime tourist attraction. Adorned with salubrious climate, green landscapes and superb natural beauty, it beckons the tourist.

WORTH VISITING PLACES OF MANIPUR

Shri Shri Govindajee Temple : This temple adjacent to the palace of the former rulers of Manipur, is a sacred center for Vaisnavites. It is a simple and beautiful structure with twin gold domes, a paved courtyard and a large congregation hall. The presiding deity, Radha Govinda is flanked by idols of Balaram and Krishna on one and Jagannath, Balabhadra and Subhadra on the other.

Shaheed Minar : The imposing Minar of Bir Tikendrajit park standing tall in the eastern side of the Imphal Pologround of the state's capital commemorates the indomitable spirit of Manipur martyrs who sacrificed their lives while fighting against the British in 1891. The eye-catching Minar also serves as an ideal background for photo shoots.

War Cemetery : The British and the Indian Army Cemeteries commemorating those who died in the Second World War are serene and well maintained with little stone markers and bronze plaques recording brief accounts of their anguish and sacrifice. These graves are maintained by the Commonwealth War Graves commossion.

Khwairamband Bazar or IMA Market : A unique all women's market, having 3000 "Imas" or mothers who run the stalls. This is a large crowded market at the heart of Imphal city. The market is exclusive in the sense that all the stalls are managed by women. It is split into two sections on either side of the road. Vegetables, fruit, fish and household groceries are sold on one side and exquisite handlooms and household tools on the other. Not far away is a street where beautiful Manipuri wicker works and basketry are sold.

Manipur Zoological Garden : About 6 kms from Imphal towards the west, lies the Zoological Garden at Iroishemba, hidden half-a-mile from the Imphal-Kangchup road. Graceful brow-antlered deer (Sangai), one of the rarest species in the world, can be seen there in sylvan surroundings. A trip to this garden at the foot of pine-covered hillocks in the western-most corner of Lamphelpat will be an affair to remember.

Manipur State Museum : This interesting museum near the Polo Ground has a fairly good display of Manipur's tribal heritage and a collection of portraits of Manipur's former rulers. Particularly interesting items are costumes, arms & weapons, relics and historical documents.

Khonghampat Orchidarium : Seven kilometres from Imphal on Highway No. 39 is the Central Orchidarium, which covers 200 acres and houses over 110 rare varieties of orchids, which include almost a dozen endemic species. The peak blooming season of this orchidarium is March-April.

Singda : At an altitude of 921 metres, Singda is a beautiful picnic spot 16 kms away from Imphal. The scenery is inviting. There is an Inspection Bunglow to convenience visitors. Greeted by a breeze-ruffled artificial lake, every visitor is tempted to revisit the spot.

Kangchup is a beautiful health resorts on the hills overlooking the Manipur Valley. The site is picturesque and worth seeing. With the construction of Singda Dam at Kangchup, the place has become one of the important picnic spots.

Langthabal : It is 6 kms from Imphal on the Indo-Myanmar road. Langthabal is a small hillock rich in the relics of an old historical place, well-planned tempted to attract the tourists.

Red Hill (Maibam Lokpa Ching) : It is a hillock about 17 kms South of Imphal City on Tiddim Road. The place was an action-packed location where a fierce battle took place between the Allied Forces and the Japanese Forces in World War II. Japanese war veterans constructed a monument at the foot of this hill and it was significantly named "India Peace Memorial"

Bishnupur : Bishnupur is 27 kms away from Imphal City on Tiddim Road. Here stands the conical temple of lord Vishnu built in 1467 during the region of King Kyamba. It is interesting because of its antiquity and architectural design which was influenced by Chinese style. Bishnupur is also known for its stoneware production. The bustling district headquaters is popular for hill-grown oranges, yongchak (tree-bean) and vegetables. Shoibum (fermented bamboo-shoot) scents the air around the town market.

Loukoipat : It is a hot-favourite tourist spot in Bishnupur district lying just in the outskirts of the district headquarters. A small but aesthetically satiating lake surrounded on all sides by green foliage-rich hillocks, is the main attraction of the spot. Boating facility is also provided to the tourists. A cool greenery-hedged is built on an elevated site overlooking the lake awaits to host visitors on the look-out for a night's stay.

Loktak Lake : Loktak lake is like a miniature sea. It is the largest fresh water lake in the North-East. Sendra is a hillock of an island of Loktak lake, 48 kms away from Imphal City on Tiddim Road. From the Tourist bunglow, set atop Sendra island, visitors can get a birds eye-view of the unique Loktak Lake and the floating mass called "Phumdis".

Phubala : A charming resort on the western fringes of the Loktak lake is situated 40 kms south of Imphal. It is joined to the mainland by a low causeway. From there, life in and around the gigantic expanse of the Loktak lake can be viewed vividly.

Moirang : Moirang is located 45 kms away from Imphal city on Tiddim Road. The ancient temple of the pre-Hindu deity, Lord Thangjing stands there. Every May, men and women in bright traditional costumes sing and dance in honour of the lord there in an eventful festival called Moirang Lai Haraoba.

Keibul Lamjao National Park : The Park is located in the south western part of the Loktak lake. This is the last natural habitat of the marsh-friendly brow-antlered deer (Sangai) of Manipur. Keibul Lamjao National Park is the only floating park in the world.

Kaina : It is a beautiful hillock about 29 kms from Imphal on Imphal-Yairipok Road. Kaina is a sacred place of the Hindus. According to legend, one night, Shri Govindajee appeared to his devotee Bhagyachandra, Maharaja of Manipur, in a dream and asked him to build a temple enshrined with his image carved out of a Jackfruit tree which was then growing at Kaina. Hill shrubs and natural surroundings give the place a saintly solemnity. Ceremonial dances depicting the divine dream are performed as Rasa Lila at the Mandop.

Khongjom : It is situated on the Indo-Myanmar Road, 36 kms away from Imphal. It is a place of utmost historical importance. Khonjom was the venue where Major General Paona Brajabashi and other brave Manipuri warriors proved their worth in warfare against the mighty force of the invading British Army in 1891. Khongjom is regarded in awe as a symbol of patriotism and valour. A war memorial laid on the top of this venerable hill adds the historical ambience of the heroic site. Khongjom Day is observed as a State Function every year on April 23.

Andro : Andro lies 27 kms east of the state capital Imphal. The small town is an ancient Scheduled Caste village of the state. A cultural complex was established there by the Mutua Museum, Imphal. It exhibited potteries of the North-eastern region of India. There also is a Doll-house wherein dolls of recognized Tribes of the State are displayed.

Churachandpur : It is the second biggest town of the state spreading out on both sides of the Tiddim Road, 60 kms away from Imphal. It exhibited potteries of the North-Eastern region of India.

Tengnoupal : 69 kms away from Imphal on the Indo-Myanmar highway, one comes across the highest point in altitude on the way to Moreh, the border town with Myanmar. Over there, one is at advantage point to have a full view of the valley portion of the state. To stay at or pass through the elevated peak of a village, warm clothes are needed in any part of the year. You'll feel as if you are put inside a fridge. As in Ooty, summer is gone from Tengnoupal.

Moreh : The international border town is located on the Indo-Myanmar Road 110 kms south east of Imphal. Being a commercial town, it attracts a large number of people away from Tamu, its Myanmarese counterpart which was of late given face lift. The recent opening of the Border Trade turned Moreh into an important commercial hub in the North-East. Right on the other side of the border, at Namphalong, there's a big Myanmarese shopping complex selling all kinds of Thailand and Chinese consumer goods. The shopping complex serves as a poor man's alternative to Bangkok's National Stadium Shopping Arcade. Things come much cheaper there. Conducted Tours are organized from Moreh to Myanmarese towns like Kalimiew and Mandalay. Such a tour is of the rare opportunities.

Ukhrul : The district headquarters of Ukhrul district is situated 83 kms away from Imphal in the east. Undoubtedly, one of the highest hill stations of the state, Ukhrul is famous for a peculiar type of terrestrial Lily, the Siroy Lily (Lilium macklinae sealy) which is grown on the Siroy Hill. Khangkhui Lime Caves are interesting places for excursion. Ukhrul wears gay and festive appearance during Christmas. Known for the natural hospitality of its people, it is the place where pioneer missionary, William Pettigrew was first offered a foothold.

Tamenglong : It's the district headquaters of Tamenglong district situated 156 kms from Imphal. The region is known for its deep gorges, mysterious caves, refreshing waterfalls, exotic orchids and oranges. The Tharon Caves, Booming Meadow, Zeilad Lake and Barak waterfalls are interesting tourist spots in Tamenglong district. There's nothing to beat the Tamenglong brand of oranges and cane-mats.

Koubru Leikha : Koubru is one of the pious mountains of Manipur and is located on NH-39. A three hundred years old temple of Lord Koubru Mahadeva is situated in the foot hills of "Awang asuppa yoimyai khunda ahanba mountain". The devotees offer rituals in the name of Koubra Baba or the Lord Shiva.

Waithout Lake : 16 kms on Indo-Myanmar Road a picturesque site famous for its pineapple slopes. A tourist lodge at the fringe of the lake.

Khoupum Valley : It is a very beautiful small valley with flat land of about 8 sq. miles (20.72 sq. kms). It is situated on the Old Cachar Road, roughly half way between Bishenpur and Jirighat.

Langol : It is scenic spot situated in the north-western part of Imphal town. The sprawling game villages with the overlooking ranges of hill is worth visiting. Temples of Thongak Lairembi, Langol Lairembi, Viswanath Mandir, Nature care Hospital, Shija Hospital etc. are located here.

Nupee Lal Memorial & Complex : It is built to perpetuate the memory of Nupeelal (women uprings). It is located by the side of Imphal Head post office. One can see photographs, records of the events displayed in this splendor memorial buildings.

Kanchup : It is a serene place lying on some enchanting hills with much beautiful scenary. The scheme of water works at it is quite enthralling to witness.

ADVENTURE TOURISM

Adventure Tourism facilities are also being developed at the Manipur Mountaineering and Trekking Association (MMTA) Complex at Lamdan (Sudarshan Park) near the Loktak Hydroelectric Power Project, the Manipur Adventure and Allied Sports Institute (MAASI) Complex at Keirao and at the Tourist Home located in the Siroi Hills near Ukhrul District Headquarters. These Associations conduct training and treks for tourists with an adventurers streak. They also offer opportunities for jungle exploration, mountaineering, rock climbing, etc.

MAJOR TOURIST PLACES : AT A GLANCE

❖ **RELIGIOUS :**	1. Koubru Leikha 2. Andro 3. Shree Shree Govindajee Temple 4. Kaina
❖ **HISTORICAL :**	1. INA Memorial (Moirang) 2. Khongjom 3. Andro 4. War Cemetery (Indian and British) 5. Shaheed Minar 6. Bishnupur 7. Canchipur 8. Langthabal 9. Red Hill
❖ **HILL STATION :**	1. Tamenglong 2. Mao 3. Tengnoupal 4. Ukhrul
❖ **IMPORTANT TOWN :**	1. Churachandpur 2. Imphal 3. Moreh
❖ **WILDLIFE :**	1. Keibul Lamjao National Park 2. Manipur Zoological Garden
❖ **SCENIC :**	1. Loukoipat 2. Phubala 3. Khonghampat Orchidarium 4. Khangkhui cave 5. Loktak lake and its isles 6. Waithou lake 7. Kangchup and Singda dam
❖ **MUSEUM :**	1. INA Museum 2. Sekta Archaeological Living Museum 3. Manipur State Museum 4. Andro

TRANSPORT

The state of Manipur is well depended on Roads for its transportation. Aviation has its own share while the Railways is still in his early days of life, as far as Manipur is concern.

ROADS

Imphal, the capital of Manipur is joined by road (NH-39) with Nagaland on the north and Myanmar on the east, on the west with Assam by NH-53 and Mizoram on the south by NH-150.

The state Highways and major district roads form the secondary road system and take care of collection and distributary functions. The length of surfaced road of National Highway was 1,317 Kms in 2013 which was the same as in the previous year. On the other hand, the other roads like State Highways, PWD Roads, Rural Road, Urban Road and Project Road have changed over the years. The length of road according to category is presented in Table below:

Length of Road in Manipur

(In kms.)

Classification of Road	2012		2013	
	Total	**Surfaced**	**Total**	**Surfaced**
(1)	**(2)**	**(3)**	**(4)**	**(5)**
National Highways	1317	1317	1317	1317
State Highways	1137	1137	715	620
PWD Roads	8305	3475	9404	3407
Rural Road	6680	2964	7635	3919
Urban Road	212	156	166	111
Project Road	1600	1408	1601	1601

3 National Highways : *(i)* NH-39, *(ii)* NH-53 and *(iii)* NH-150 criss-cross the State connecting all Districts. Imphal the capital of Manipur is joined by NH-39 with Nagaland on the North and Myanmar on the east, on the west with Assam by NH-53 and Mizoram on the south by NH-150.

The Saurashtra-Silchar Super Highway Project is being extended to Moreh. With the proposed Moreh to Mae Sot (Thailand) Highway coming up, Manipur will become the gateway to South-East Asia.

NH-39 : It is also known as Indo-Myanmar Road or Dimapur Road. It is the most important national highway of Manipur. It is a life line of Manipur. Its total length is 215 kms. The nearest rail station at Dimapur (Nagaland) could be reached only through this road.

NH-53 : It is also known as New Cachar Road. It connects Imphal with Jirighat in Cachar District of Assam. Its total length is 225 kms.

NH-150 : The National Highway No. 150 will be another National Highway running through Manipur. It is the road connecting Jessami–Ukhrul–Imphal–Churachand–Tipaimukh with Aizwal of Mizoram. Manipur's share of the proposed NH-150 would be 523 km long.

AVIATION

Imphal Airport is the second largest airport in the North Eastern Region. Imphal is connected to Agartala, Aizwal, Dimapur, Guwahati, Kolkata, Pune, Silchar, Bengaluru and New Delhi by Indian Airlines, Jet Airways, Indigo and Air Deccan and Alliance Air. New flights from carrier like Spicejet. Imphal Airport is being upgraded into the status of International Airport for which process of land acquisition work has already been taken up. The construction of infrastructure for Night Landing Facility at Imphal airport has been completed and Night Flights have started. A "dedicated airline" for NE Region, particularly for connectivity within the NE States is under consideration of NEC/DoNER.

RAILWAYS

The State is included in the railway map of India with the opening of a rail head at Jiribam in May 1990. A railway line of 50 km connects it with Silchar (Assam) railway station. It is 255 km from Imphal. Dimapur, 215 km from Imphal is the nearest rail-head.

The Jiribam - Tupul Railway line has been declared as a National Project. Construction of the Line is in good progress.

AGRICULTURE

Agriculture and allied activities are the only mainstay of the State's economy where about 70 per cent of the population depends on it. The State has two topographical zones—valley and hills. The valley is known as the 'Rice Bowl' of the State. The valley has sub-tropical to tropical to sub-temperate climate. The hills have sub-temperate to temperate climate with an average altitude of 3000 metres above MSL. The State has distinct winter, warm, humid and rainy summer. The average rainfall during the last 10 years is 1482.20 mm. with heavy precipitation during the month of June, July and August. The growth of agriculture in the State has been quite uneven for the reason that its production still depends on seasonal rainfall.

During the 12th Five Years Plan and Annual Plan 2015-16 thrusts is given to get self-security in food grains, oilseeds, sugarcane and potato. The Strategy for agricultural development during 12th Plan over the anticipated achievement of 2014-15.

PRINCIPAL CROPS, VEGETABLES AND FRUITS

Rice, wheat, maize, oil seeds, potato and sugarcane etc. are the main crops in the State. Among these crops, cultivation of paddy is the largest both in the plains and hills, and covers 82% of the total cultivated area. Among the variety of rice, there are two varieties of rice locally named as "CHAKHAO POIREITON" having its natural colour (dark violet) and a distinct flavor and "CHAKHAO" having its natural white colour, scent and distinctive flavor. Next to paddy, maize is the second largest cultivated crop. It occupies about 40% of the gross cropped area and grown mainly in the hills.

HORTICULTURE

The Department of Horticulture & Soil Conservation, Manipur have identified 2,77,064 hactares as potential area for growing different horticulture crops like Fruit, Vegetable, Spices, Root & Tuber crops, Aromatic & Medicinal plants etc. The area under horticulture in the state is 44,335 hactares.

Tropical and Sub-tropical Fruits

Among fruits, Banana, Pineapple and Citrus take a major share in area and production. The other fruits which are grown in sizeable area are Guava, Papaya etc. Banana is native to this region (Tamenglong).

Pineapple is mostly grown on hill slopes as rainfed crop. Giant Kew and Queen are the two leading varieties being grown.

Temperate fruits

Peach, pear and plum are being grown successfully on higher altitudes mostly low chilling varities, are performing well.

Pear : Leconte, Smith, Keifer, Coslin etc.
Peach : Flordasum, Shane-Punjab, Sharbati.
Plum : Santa Rosa, Doris, Mariposa.

Vegetables

The scenario in vegetable is much more promising in Manipur. Low productivity in most of the vegetable crops grown is directly connected to the use of genetically inferior varieties coupled with low input farming and incidence of insect pests and diseases. Several improved and high yielding varieties and F1 hybrids are now available for large scale adoption. In Manipur the valley land, after the harvest of paddy, is being successfully utilized for large scale cultivation of vegetables. Now the farmers have started using F1 and high yielding varieties.

The state abounds in cucurbitaceous vegetables like Pumpkin, Bottle gourd, Ridge gourd, Cucumber and Dolichos, Vigna, Phosphocarpus and Phaseolous and Phaseolous vulgaris (French bean). Among solanaceous vegetables, brinjal, tomato, chillies and capsicum hold great promise. In cole crops, Cabbage and cauliflower are grown in limited area. Among exotic vegetables, brussels sprout and broccoli also hold good promise due to favourable climatic conditions but these are not popular among the farmers.

FLORICULTURE

The suitable agro-climatic conditions of the state clearly indicate that wide range of ornamental crops can be grown, which can improve the economic conditions of the growers. The most promising flowers, which grow extremely well in different parts of the state are Gladiolus, Lillies, Chrysanthenum, Roses, Anthurium, Gerbera, Dahlia etc. Special mention may be made about orchids. Cymbidium, Paphiopedilum, Dendrobium are in great demand and can be successfully grown. Siroi Lilly is endemic to Manipur, however, there is no perceptible area under floriculture as it is confined to courtyard of the houses, government institutions etc.

FISHERIES

Fish is the main food item of the majority of the people in the State, particularly the Meiteis who are mainly concentrated in the valley.

FISHERY RESOURCES

The State has no marine fisheries. It has vast potential of fisheries resources comprising ponds, tanks, natural lakes, marshy areas, swampy areas, rivers, reservoirs, submerged cropped land, low lying paddy fields etc. The largest source of fish is the Loktak Lake.

The total water area in Manipur State have shrunk from around 1,00,000 ha. in 1990 to around 56,461.5 ha. in 2009-10. About 18,000 ha of water areas have been brought under fish culture operation.

The swamps and marshy areas are lying barren without any effective utilisation. The lakes, reservoirs, beels, tanks, canals, etc. cover an area of about 13,221.45 ha. whereas rivers, streams etc. account for 13,888.27 ha.

These swamps can be profitably utilized for culture of various indigeneous natural fishes such as Ukabi (Anabas tesdudineus), Ngamu (Lata fish), Ngaton (Labeo bata), Ngakrijou (Lepidocephalichthys SPP), Sareng Khoibi (Botia SPP), Nganap (Pengia SPP), Ngatin (Labeo Pangusia), Ngakra (Barbus tor), Ngasang (Esomus denricus), Phabounga (Puntius SPP), Ngamhai (Chanda SPP), Pengba (Osteobrama belangeri) etc.

FISH PRODUCTS

The production of fish in Manipur for the year 2015-16 was estimated to be 31.99 thousand tonnes as against 30.59 thousand tonnes in 2010-11. The per capita production of fish for 2014-15 was 8.08 kgs as compared to the estimated per capita requirements of 10.50 kgs., registering a shortfall of 2.42 kgs. per head per annum and the per capita production fish for 2010-11 was 8.01 kgs. as compared to the estimated per capita requirements at 10.50 kgs., with a short fall of 2.49 kgs. per head per annum.

The total requirement of fish far exceeds its indigenous production. Large quantities of fishes are being imported from outside the State every year to fill this gap. The estimated requirement of fish for the year 2004-2005 was 23.00 thousand tonnes whereas the actual fish production was 17.80 thousand tonnes. This huge gap is to be met by harnessing the vast fishery resources of State by adopting advanced scientific techniques of fish culture and consolidating the available infrastructures already laid and by introducing new schemes and projects. This will enable to meet not only the requirement of fish in the State but also for export to neighbouring States like Assam, Nagaland, Mizoram and even to the neighbouring country, Myanmar.

GOVT. FISH FARMS IN MANIPUR

Sl.No.	*District*	*Name of Fish Farm*
1.	Imphal West	D.L.F.S.F. Lamphel
2.	Imphal East	F.R.C. Khudrakpam
3.	Thoubal	D.L.F.S.F. Wangbal
4.	Thoubal	Waithou E.F.F.
5.	Bishnupur	D.F.F.S.F. Ningthoukhong.
6.	Bishnupur	Regional Pengba Seed Farm Haotak
7.	Bishnupur	Takmu E.F.F. Takmu
8.	Senapati	D.L.F.S.F. Keithelmanbi
9.	Senapati	Cold Water Fish Farm, Molhoi
10.	Ukhrul	Mirang Fish Seed Farm
11.	Chandel	Fish Seed Farm, Komlathabi
12.	Chandel	Fish Seed Farm, Khambathel
13.	Churachandpur	Fish Seed Farm, Phailian
14.	Churachandpur	Fish Seed Farm, Tuibong
15.	Tamenglong	Fish Seed Farm, Tamenglong
16.	Tamenglong	Fish Seed Farm, Khoupum
17.	Jirbam Sub Disn	Fish Seed Farm, Patchao
18.	Jiribam Sub Division	Compite Fish Farm, Kutikhong

MAJOR FISH FARMERS DEVELOPMENT AGENCIES

1. Fish Farmers Development Agency, Imphal
2. Fish Farmers Development Agency, Thoubal
3. Fish Farmers Development Agency, Bishnupur
4. Fish Farmers Development Agency, Ukhrul
5. Fish Farmers Development Agency, Senapati
6. Fish Farmers Development Agency, Tamenglong
7. Fish Farmers Development Agency, Churachandpur
8. Fish Farmers Development Agency, Chandel

FOOD AND FLAVOUR

The traditional Manipuri fine dining was a literally 'sit-down' affair with banana-leaf plates. Their love for rice can be seen in every household. Some take rice with meat, and some others prefer a fish delicacy along with the main dish. In fact Kabok, a traditional speciality, is mostly fried rice with a world of vegetables added in. The Iromba, an eclectic combination of fish, vegetables and bamboo shoots is served fermented. Along with all these, Manipuri menu of food and flavour contains many other delicious items. Some of them are given below:

- Heithongba is a pungent dish of lemon, sugar, salt, amla (Indian gooseberry) or tamarind.
- Moroi Morok Thongba, meaning different types of vegetables or 'little plants', is another speciality. Morok stands for green chillies so this dish may be a bit hot to taste.
- Madhur Jhan is a sweet made of milk, sugar and gram flour.
- Manipuri cuisine is a unique experience in itself. Their vegetarian thali is famous.
- A black lentil called Uti is compulsory at all feasts.
- A dessert made of rice called Chak Sao is deep violet in colour and is combined with milk, sugar, coconut and dry fruits.
- Suktani is a combination of neem leaves, basak leaves and sugar.
- Sweet Kabok, made up of molasses and rice, is a famous name among the Manipuris.
- Fish is also an important part of Manipuri cuisine and is cooked in numerous ways.
- The drink called shekmai, made in a village with the same name, is a famous country wine of the state.
- **Chicken Chatni :** Simple boiled chicken mixed with chilli, ginger, native onion and spices.
- **Hancham :** Known in Mietei dialect as champhut, it is simple boiled vegetables without any spices.
- **Khamui :** Baked bread with special sticky rice. There are two methods of preparation; one is fried and the other is baked into cakes then wrap with panama or cardamom leaves and boiled.
- **Vaitei :** Ordinarily known as Khor, it is prepared with floured rice (sticky rice) made to ferment in a jar-filled water with floured sprouted-paddy grains.
- **Chakhan :** For those who don't relish the above drinks, simple fully boiled sticky rice with some soluble sweetening items are used.
- **Chathur :** Preparation, same as Vaitei as also the materials, but let to cool and ferment. This is used as cold drink.

MASS MEDIA

In a country like India, mass communication plays an important role in creating people's awareness about national policies and programmes by providing information and education, besides healthy entertainment. It helps people to be active partners in the nation-building endeavour. Same is the case with the state of Manipur. Respective state ministry and departments, with the co-operation of Ministry of Information and Broadcasting, Govt. of India, are working for the development of wide colourful culture of this north-eastern paradise. All India Radio, Doordarshan and local newspapers and magazines are some of the vital sources of communication here.

A.I.R. & DOORDARSHAN

First Manipuri Programme was broadcast through AIR Gauhati for a period of 45 minutes only daily. It was somewhere around 1957-58. But, for Manipuri programmes, it was not too far away from their own station when All India Radio, Imphal commenced its public service broadcasting with a modest setup on 15th August 1963 under the station directorship of R.K. Acharya. Initially, it was consisting of a pilot studio and a 200 watt Medium wave (MW) transmitter. Within a couple of years, it was augmented to a one killowatt (kw) transmitter. This transmitter enabled AIR to cover Imphal town and surrounding villages only. The pilot studio was housed in the present Raj Bhavan complex and the transmitter in the DM college campus. To cover the entire state of Manipur, a 50 KW MW high power transmitter was commissioned near the Mayang Imphal village in a site measuring 34.5 acres in October 1972. This improved the coverage of the station substantially to an extent of 75% of the area of Manipur state. Studio center was shifted to present location at Palace compound during 1980. Captive generators have been provided at the studio complex for operating the studios and FM transmitter. Studio setup consists of a drama, music and talk studio along with dubbing room and control room. Consider in still there are number of uncovered packets in the hill terrain, a SW transmitter of 50 kw was installed and commissioned on 1992 at Mayang Imphal center. Presently, AIR is successfully disseminating the state's culture and values through its wide reach.

From January 29, 2004, a Manipur Programme called 'LEIKOL' is being broadcast in AIR Delhi under the Bhasha Bharati Programme.

On the other hand first Doordarshan (TV) Kendra of Manipur was started on 30th April 1992 from Porompat, while the more entertaining version of Doordarshan, Metro Channel, was started on 23rd December, 1995.

NEWSPAPERS & JOURNALS

Having situated in the easternmost corner of India, the wave of journalism could be felt only in the early part of 1920s. It is believed that, newspapers published from Calcutta have a great influence on the masses thereby signalling the idea of journalism in the state of Manipur. It may be pointed out that, geographical isolation, communication bottleneck, backwardness of the people may be some of the reasons for the lackadaisical development of the forth estate in Manipur.

History has it that, 'Meitei Chanu' was the first print journal in Manipur. It was edited by Hijam Irabot Singh during 1925-26. However, the journal could not survived long and it vanished away from the news stand after 5/6 issues were brought out. In 1933, another paper 'Dainik Manipur' was published under the editorship of Gokulchandra at the Churachand Printing Press. The paper was believed to be widely read not only in Manipur but also in Assam and neighbouring states. The publication discussed about religions, custom and traditions and political structure of the time. The newspaper, with a daily circulation of about 1,000 copies was known for its critical views against the then British Government in Manipur. The result was that, the newspaper had to be closed after five years of publication under the diktat of the Government.

In 1937, yet another newspaper 'Manipur Matam' was published from Tarun Press. The paper, edited by Rajkumar Shitaljit Singh hardly survived for about three years. It has a circulation of around 300 copies a day and was also believed to be circulated in Assam. By the early parts of 1939, a bi-weekly paper 'Manipur Paojel' was launched in Manipur. In those days, cases against journalists were not uncommon. Because of the Press in Manipur were a part of the Freedom Movement, the Government of the day came down heavily on them. K. Kunjabihari, an independent journalist was summoned by the Manipur Darbar and Sadar Panchayat. He became the first ever journalist in the State to have been put under bar. Due to a strong stand taken by the then British Government against the press, publication of newspaper/magazines were virtually impossible in those days. However, a concerted effort were made to bring out newspaper/magazine against all odds. In 1948, one year after India won her Freedom, a weekly magazine 'Praja' was published under the editorship of Loitam Yaima. A new chapter of journalism was witnessed after India won Independence from the British rule.

STATEHOOD AND THE PRESS

The State of Manipur witnessed a sudden increase of newspapers and magazines after the attainment of full-fledged state in 1972. There was a big wave of journalism brewing in all parts of the State. The people of Manipur, particularly the 'hoi polloi' started to understand the importance of media in development process. Awareness among the public was visibly increasing. A new gear of media spirit was added to the journalists' community following the attainment of statehood. It is, therefore, no surprising to see the number of newspapers and magazines increasing by leaps and bounds. In the process, a new trend of journalism took its shape with political parties taking keen interest in media.

FIRST IN NEWSPAPERS AND MAGAZINES

Newspapers/ Magazines	Name of the Publication (Year)	First Editor
❖ First Manipuri magazine	Meitei Leima (1917-18)	A. Thambou Singh
❖ First daily newspaper	Dainik Manipur Patrika (1932)	Gokulchandra Singh
❖ First journal	Meitei Chanu (1922)	Hijam Irabot
❖ First English journal	Meitei Leirang (1969)	—
❖ First weekly magazine	Praja (1948)	Loitman Yaima
❖ First bi-weekly newspaper	Manipur Paojel (1939)	K. Kunjabihari
❖ First Health journal	Meitei Maiba	Sagolsem Indramani

FILM & DRAMA

Manipur's first produced film, 'Meipak, Son of Manipur', was a documentry. It was released in 1972. However, the first attempted Manipuri film of Manipur was 'Mainu Pemcha'. A part of it was made in 1948-49 but unfortunately remaining parts of this movie could not be completed. On the other hand the beginning of staging Drama in Manipuri Language (Meeteilon) may be said to have first started from the year 1914 when students of Johnstone High School, Imphal staged a Drama called **Arjungi Maithiba** (Partha Parajay) in one of the earliest Manipuri Dramas that won First position in All India Drama Competition in 1954 was M.D.U's "Haorang Leishang Saphabee".

FIRST IN MANIPURI FILM AND DRAMA

❖	First Manipuri Feature Film	: Matamgi Manipur (9th April 1972) Directed by : Debkumar Bose
❖	First Manipuri Coloured Movie	: Langlen Thadoi (1984) Directed by : Kh. Pramodini
❖	First Manipuri Documentary Film	: Maipak–the Son of Manipur (November 9, 1971) Directed: Debkumar Bose
❖	First Manipuri-Full length Feature Film	: Langlen Thadoi (1984) Directed by : Kh. Pramodini
❖	First Manipuri Film Producer	: Karam Manmohan Singh (K.T. Films).
❖	First Manipuri Film Director	: S.N. Chand
❖	First Manipuri Film Actor	: Robindro Sharma
❖	First Manipuri Film Actress	: Rashi Devi
❖	First Manipuri Film to receive the best Feature Film Award in the Manipur State Film Festival	: Imagee Ningthem (1981) Directed by : Aribam Shyam Sharma
❖	First Manipuri Feature Film in direct 35 mm colour format	: Madhabee (1993) Directed by : L. Banka Sharma
❖	First Manipur Child to get the Best Child Actor Award	: Leikhendra Singh (At 8 years of age)
❖	First Manipuri Film to receive the best documentary film in the non-feature category in the first Manipur State Film Festival	: Sanaleibak Manipur (1980) Directed by : Aribam Shyam Sharma
❖	First Manipuri Documentary Film to be ever screened publicly	: Meipak the son of Manipur (1997) Directed by : Debkumar Bose
❖	First Manipuri Film, which is also the first Indian film to receive the prestigious "Grand Prix" at the Nante International Film Festival.	: Imagee Ningthem (1982). Directed by : Aribam Shyam Sharma
❖	First Manipuri film to be screened in Indian Panorama	: Matamgi Manipur
❖	First Manipuri Film to receive the President's Medal in the 20th National Film Festival	: Matamgi Manipur (1972).
❖	First Attempted Manipuri Feature Film	: Mainu Pemcha (Around the year 1948-49)
❖	Pioneer Film Making Organisation of Manipur	: Shree Shree Govindajee Film Company (Estd. 1946-47).
❖	Pioneer Film Society of Manipur	: Manipuri Film Society (Estd. 1966)
❖	First Manipuri play	: Narasingha (1925)
❖	Manipur's first permanent theatre house	: Manipur Friends Dramatic Union (1930)

Manipur Film Development Corporation

It is an autonomous body set for the promotion and development of film industry in the state of Manipur. It regularly organizes National Film Festivals etc. and perform many activities for the promotion of film industry in Manipur. It is located at Palace Compound, Imphal.

SPORTS

Sagol Kangjei (Manipuri Polo) : The Sagol Kangjei has been adapted and adopted by the international enthusiasts of the game as Polo and now it's now being played worldwide. Today, the world has accepted that the game of Polo originated from Manipur. The Manipuri Polo is played with seven players (in each side) who mount and ride ponies, which are usually 4/5 feet in height. Each player is fitted with Polo-stick made of bamboo root. The mounted player gallop after the ball to hit it straight into the goal. Extremely masculine and vigour-taxing, the exhilarating game is now played in two styles—the pana or original Manipur style and the international style i.e. Polo. It is heart-cheering to see Manipuri players in their sixties and even seventies riding ponies at full gallop playing Sagol Kangjei (polo) with gusto. The ponies are also decorated fully with various guards of protecting the eyes, forehead, flanks etc.

The game was much flourished in the reign of King Kyamba who ruled between 1467 and 1508 and king Khogemba who reigned between 1597 and 1652. The Britishers learnt the nuances of the game of Sagol Kangjei in the 19th century from Manipur and after that clever refinement, the erstwhile indigenous game was renamed Polo and played in other parts of the globe.

Khong Kangjei (Manipuri Hockey) : It is also a very popular Manipuri game. The game is played with seven players on either side and each player is equipped with a bamboo stick about 4 feet in length which is bended at the lower tip like the modern hockey stick. The ball is started with a throw of the bamboo-root-made ball in a field of 200 × 80 yards. A player may carry the ball in any manner towards the goal but he shall have to score a goal only by hitting the ball with his stick. There are no goal posts. A goal is scored when the ball crosses the goal-line fully. A player often encounters an opponent in his attempt at carrying or hitting the ball toward the goal. The encounter may develop into a tussling trial of strength which is indigenously known as Mukna. The game is actually an admixture of football, hockey, rugby and wrestling.

Yubi Lakpi (Manipuri Rugby) : "Yubi" in Manipur means coconut and "Lakpi" means snatching. The oriental game is played on the lush green turf of the palace ground or at the Bijoy Govinda Temple ground. Each side has 7 players in a field that is about 45 × 18 metres in area one side of which forms the central portion of the goal line. The coconut serves the purpose of a ball and is offered to the king or the judges who sit just beyond the goal line.

Hiyang Tannaba (Boat Race) : It is generally held in the month of November at Thangapat(Moat). The boats called Hiyang Hiren are regarded to be invested with spiritual powers and the game is associated with religious rites. The Meiteis believe that worship of the Hiyang Hiren will prevent one from evil omens. The rowers wear traditional dresses and head-gears. The game is also conducted during spells of natural calamity.

Kaang : Played on the mud floor of a big out house fixed targets hit with "Kang" which is a flat and oblong instrument made of either ivory or lac. Normally each team has 7 male partners. The game is also played as a mixed doubles contest. Played strictly during the period between 'Cheiraoba' (Manipuri New Year's day) and the Rath Yatra festival. Manipuri religiously adhere to its time-frame as popular belief holds that if the game is played beyond its given limit, evil spirits invade the mind of players and spectators.

Thang-Ta & Sarit Sarat : These are the forms of Manipuri Martial Arts, the traditions of which had been passed down over the centuries. They are energy-consuming and skill demanding arts of fighting. The indigenous martial art-forms were meant to hone one's battle-craft during peace times in the olden days when Manipuri war warrior required to serve his country at war-times. A martial-artist has to undergo strenuous pratice sessions. Only the brave and the athletic could excel. The art, as seen today, observes elaborate rituals and rules, which are strictly followed by the participants.

Mukna (Manipuri Wrestling) : It is also a very popular oldest game of Manipuri's. Mukna has been in vogue since the existence of Manipuri society. It is a trial of strength using sheer physical force. The game is part of a ceremonial function and enjoyed due patronage in the olden days. The game requires enduring physical stamina, speed and agility. In the olden days, players excelling in the game received royal favours and prizes. Whereas, it is survival of the fattest in Japanese Sumo-wrestling, it is survival of the fittest for Mukna.

Besides these, there are some other interesting games like Lamjel (foot-race), Mangjong (broad jump), Uraobi (Manipuri Kabbadi), Seboti (aerobic game style), Chenjong, Phibulhabi and Amangoi etc.

OLYMPIANS FROM MANIPUR

Since 1984, Manipur has consistently been a part of Indian Olympic squad. Some of the well-known Olympians from Manipur are:

Neel Komol Singh : He was the first Manipuri's Olympian, participated in Los Angeles, 1984 as a goal keeper of Indian Hockey team.

Thoiba Sing : Thoiba was a skilled forward hockey player. He participated in the 1988 Olympics at Seoul, South Korea.

Sanamacha Chanu : A weightlifter from Manipur who got the 6th position in 2000 Sydney Olympics. She also represented the state and nation in Athens Olympics, 2004.

Brojeshwori Devi : She was another Manipuri girl participated in Sydney games in 2000. She was the only women Judo player participant of India and reached upto 3rd round.

N. Dingko Singh : Boxer from Manipur participated in Sydney Olympics. Dingko Singh was also an Asian gold medalist.

N. Kunjarani Devi : Weightlifter, got the 4th position in Athens Olympics, 2004. She had also won the Gold medal in 2006, Melbourne Commonwealth Games.

M.C. Mary Kom : Women boxer from manipur who won the bronze medal in 2012 London Olympics.

SPORTS AWARDS FOR MANIPUR

N. Kunjarani Devi (Weightlifting)	: First Arjuna Award winner for Manipur; also the first winner of Rajiv Gandhi Khel Ratna for Manipur.
N. Dingko Sing (Boxing)	: Arjuna Award
Sanamacha Chanu (Weightlifting)	: Arjuna Award
Tingongleima Chanu (Hockey)	: Arjuna Award
M.C. Merrycom (Boxing)	: Arjuna Award; Rajiv Gandhi Khel Ratna
Surjalata Devi (Hockey)	: Arjuna Award
Anita Chanu (Mountaineering)	: Arjuna Award
Tombi Devi (Judo)	: Arjuna Award
L. Sarita Devi (Boxing)	: Arjuna Award
Sandhya Rani (Wushu)	: Arjuna Award
Suranjoy Singh (Boxing)	: Arjuna Award
L. Bombayla Devi (Archery)	: Arjuna Award
Ng. Sonia Chanu (Weightlifting)	: Arjuna Award
M. Bimoljit Singh (Wushu)	: Arjuna Award
Y. Renubala Chanu (Weightlifting)	: Arjuna Award
Y. Sanathoi Devi (Wushu)	: Arjuna Award
Devendro Singh Laishram (Boxing)	: Arjuna Award
Oinam Bembem Devi (Football)	: Arjuna Award
Mirabai Chanu (Weightlifting)	: Rajiv Gandhi Khel Ratna
Chinglensana Singh Kangujam (Hockey)	: Arjun Award

SOME FIRSTS IN SPORTS IN MANIPUR

- The First National Games were held in Manipur in 1999 at Imphal.
- The first Manipuri Sportsperson, to take part in Olympic games is Neel Komal Singh (1984).
- The first Manipuri sportsperson to receive the "Arjuna Award" is N. Kunjarani Devi. She also became the first Manipuri sports person to receive the "Rajiv Gandhi Khel Ratna Award" in 1996-1997.
- The first Manipuri to win gold medal in "Asian Games" is Ng Ding Ko Singh (1998). He is also first Manipuri naval boxer to have won a gold medal at the international level.
- Suranjoy Singh of Manipur is the first Indian boxer to clinch a gold medal in the Intercontinental Presidents Cup.
- The first Manipuri to win medal in Olympics is M.C. Mary Kom. Manipuri star women boxer Mary Kom won bronze in London Olympics 2012.

MANIPURI SPORTSPERSONS IN ASIAN GAMES—2018

The 2018 Asian Games, officially known as the 18th Asian Games and also known as Jakarta-Palembang 2018, is a pan-Asian multisport event which were held from 18 August to 2 September 2018 in the Indonesian cities of Jakarta and Palembang.

India which ended its campaign at the Games with a total of 69 medals (G: 15, S: 24, B: 30), finished eighth both in terms of gold medals and the total tally.

Players from Manipur Gurumayum Jiteshwar Sharma, Khangembam Niken Singh, Nagathem Jotin Singh, Sorokhaibam Malemnganba Singh Thokchom Seitaram Singh, Wahengbam Henary Singh, Waikhom Sanjeck Singh and Yumnam Akash Singh won bronze medal in Sepak Takraw (Men) while Naorem Roshibina Devi won bronze medal in Wushu (Women).

MANIPURI SPORTSPERSONS IN COMMONWEALTH GAMES-2018

The 2018 Commonwealth Games, officially known as the XXI Commonwealth Games were held in Gold Coast, Australia from 4 to 15 April 2018. India finished third with 66 medals (26 Gold, 20 Silver, 20 Bronze). Three Sportspersons from Manipur Mirabai Chanu, Sanjita Chanu and Mary Kom got gold medals in the games. World champion weightlifter Mirabai Chanu won gold in the women's 48 kilogram category. Weightlifter Sanjita Chanu won gold in the women's 53 kilogram category. Mary Kom won gold in the women's 45-48 kg boxing category.

ABBREVIATIONS

(A)

AAAM : Amateur Athletic Association, Manipur
ABA : Athletic Brothers Association
AFORD : Association For Rural Development
AMESCO : All Manipur Ethnic Socio Cultural Organisation
AMFA : All Manipur Football Association
AMMIK : All Manipur Matamgi Isei Kanglup
AMSA : All Manipur Sports Association
AMSU : All Manipur Students Union
AMUCO : All Manipur United Clubs Organisation

(B)

BDO : Block Development Officer
BNU : Brachin National Union
BTI : Basic Training Institute
BOAT : Bheigachandra Open Air Theatre

(C)

CAD : Command Area Development
CEDT : Centre for Economic Design & Technology
CLAHRO : Civil Liberties and Human Rights Organisation
COHR : Committee On Human Rights

(D)

DESAM : Democratic Students Alliance of Manipur
DIC : District Industry Center
DIET : District Institute of Educational Training
DRDA : District Rural Development Authority
DRPP : Democratic Revolutionary Peoples Party

(E & F)

ESU : Eastern Sporting Union
FPM : Federal Party of Manipur

(G & H)

GAD : General Administrative Department
GM Hall : Gandhi Memorial Hall
HPC : Hmar People's Convention

(I)

IBSA : Indo Burma Sporting Association
ICEM : Institute of Competitive Examination, Manipur
IFCD : Irrigation & Flood Control Deptt.
IMA : International Manipuri Assn.

ITI : Industrial Training Institute
ISTV : Information Service T.V.
IUCB : Imphal Urban Co-operative Bank

(J)

JNMDA : Jawaharlal Nehru Manipur Dance Academy

(K)

KCP : Kangleipak Communist Party
KNA : Kuki National Army
KNF : Kuki National Front
KYKL : Kanglei Yawol Kanna Lup

(L)

LDA : Loktak Development Authority
LMSLC : Lairenmayum Seibyasachi Law College
LSTB : Lainingthou Sanamahi Temples Board

(M)

MAHUD : Municipal Administration, Housing & Urban Development
MCHALEIMA: Meitei Chanura Leishem Marup
MANIDCO : Manipur Industrial Development Corporation Ltd.
MASS : Manipur Assn. For Science and Society
MBC : Manipur Baptist Convention
MCS : Manipur Civil Service
MFPCS Ltd.: Manipur Fruit Processing and Cold Storage Society Ltd.
MFDC : Manipur Film Development Corporation
MHRC : Manipur Human Rights Commission
MOA : Manipur Olympic Association
MJS : Manipur Judicial Service
MPCC : Manipur Pradesh Congress Committee
MPLF : Manipur Peoples Liberation Front
MPS : Manipur Police Service
MPSC : Manipur Public Service Commission
MPP : Manipur People's Party
MR : Manipur Rifles
MRDWA : Manipur Richshaw Driver's Welfare Association
MSIC : Manipur Small Industries Corporation
MSKA : Manipur State Kala Akademi
MSRTC : Manipur State Road Transport Corporation
MU : Manipur University
MUTSU : Manipur University Tribal Student Union

(N)

NACO : Nambulmapal Athletic and Cultural Organization
NAMA : North America Manipuri Assn.
NC Rd. : New Cachar Road
NISA : North Imphal Sporting Association
NSCN : National Socialist Council of Nagalim

(P)

PANMYL : Pan Manipuri Youth League
PDF : Peoples Democratic Front
PLA : People's Liberation Army
PNWA : Poor and Needy Welfare Association

(R)

RAU : Rising Athletic Union
RIMS : Regional Institute of Medical Sciences
RIRDA : Regional Integrated Rural Development Agency
RPF : Revolutionary People's Front
RSU : Richshaw Service Union

(S)

SCERT : State Council of Educational Research and Training
SEWA : Service and Education for Welfare Action
SDC : Sub-Deputy Collector
SDO : Sub-Divisional Officer
SIE : State Institute of Education
SISI : Small Industries Service Institute

(T)

THAU : Thanmeiband Athletic Union
TNL : Tangkhul Naga Long
TRAU : Tiddim Road Athletic

(U)

UCM : United Committee, Manipur
UDP : United Democratic Party
UK Rd. : Uripok Kangchup Road
UNLF : United National Liberation Front
USA : United Sports Association

(V)

VEDSCO : Voluntary Educational, Development, Social and Cultural Organisation

(Y)

YAC : Yaiskul Athletic Club
YAAS : Youth Affairs and Sports
YPA : Youth Progressive Association

(Z)

ZNU : Zeliangrong Naga Union
ZRA : Zoumi Revolutionary Army
ZSU : Zeliangrong Student Union
ZYF : Zeliangrong Youth Front

SUPERLATIVES OF MANIPUR

FIRST IN MANIPUR

• **Teacher**	M.Purna Singh
• **Governor**	B.K. Nehru
• **First Lieutenant Governor**	Baleswar Prasad
• **First Union Minister**	R.K. Jaichandra
• **Speaker of Manipur Legislative Assembly**	T.C. Tiankham
• **First MP of Lok Sabha (inner)**	L. Jugeswor
• **First Lok Sabha MP (outer)**	Rishang Keishing
• **First MP of Rajya Sabha**	N.G. Tompok
• **Mr. Manipur**	Irom Leikhendra
• **First Mr. India**	N. Maipak
• **Recipient of Padma Shree Award**	Atombapu Sharma
• **Recipient of Sahitya Akademi Award**	Pacha Meitei
• **Recipient of Sangeet Natak Akademi Award**	M. Amubi Singh
• **Recipient of Arjun Award**	N. Kunjarani Devi
• **Recipient of Rajiv Khel Award**	N. Kunjarani Devi
• **Recipient of Gold Medal in Asian Games**	Dingko Singh
• **Bachelor of Laws**	L. Ibungohal Singh
• **Bachelor of Engineering**	Yambem Tombi
• **Olympian**	P. Neelkomal
• **Graduate**	S. Somerendra Singh
• **Matriculate**	W. Yumjao Singh
• **Woman MLA**	Mrs. Hangmila Saiza
• **Woman MP**	Kim Gangte
• **Woman Minister**	K. Apabi Devi
• **Doctor**	Th. Gorbadhan
• **Woman Doctor**	T.O. Bedamani Devi
• **Chief Commissioner**	Maj. Gen. Rawal Amar Singh
• **First Manipuri D.G.P.**	L. Jugeswor
• **British Political Agent**	Captain Gardon
• **Feature Film**	Matamgee Manipur
• **Colour Feature Film**	Langlen Thadoi
• **Documentary Film**	Maipak, Son of Manipur
• **Newspaper**	Dainik Manipur Patrika
• **Journal**	Meetei Chanu
• **Health Journal**	Meetei Maiba
• **English Journal**	Meetei Leirang
• **University**	Manipur University (Estd. 1980), Canchipur
• **Railway Station**	Jiribam (Estd. 1990)

AWARDS

Sahitya Akademi Awards

Authors	*Year*	*Books*
• **Pacha Meitei**	1973	Imphal Amasung Magee Isingnung-shitkiphibam (Novel)
• **N Kunjamohon**	1974	Elisha Amagi Mahac (Short Stories)
• **L Somendro**	1976	Mamang Leikai thambal Saatle (Poetry)
• **A Minaketan**	1977	Asheibagi Nityapad (Poetry)
• **GC Tongbra**	1978	Ngabong Khao (Play)
• **MK Binodeni**	1979	Boro Saheb Ongbi Sanatombi (Novel)
• **E Rajanikanta**	1981	Kalenthagi Leibaklei (Short Stories)
• **E Dinamani**	1982	Pistol Ama Kundalei Ama (Short Stories)
• **N Ibobi**	1983	Kamagi Mama Amasung Magi Aroiba Yaheep (Play)
• **L Viramani**	1984	Chekla Paikharabada (Short Stories)
• **Hijam Guno**	1985	Bir Tikendrajit road (Novel)
• **Kh. Prakash**	1986	Munggi Eshei (Short Stories)
• **E Nilakanta**	1987	Tirtha Jatra (Poetry)
• **E Sonamani**	1988	Mamangthong Lolabadi Maningthongda lak Una (Short Stories)
• **Nilbir Shastri**	1989	Tatkhraba Punshi Leipun (Short Stories)
• **Shree Biren**	1990	Mapan Naidrabasida (Poetry)
• **Y Ibomcha**	1991	Numittee Asum Thengillakli (Short Stories)
• **A Chiteswar**	1992	Tharo Sangbi (Novel)
• **Arambam Biren**	1993	Punshigi Marudhyan (Novel)
• **RK Mani**	1994	Mayai Karaba Shamu (Short Stories)
• **A Samarendra**	1995	Ieibaklei (Play)
• **RK Madhubir**	1996	Praloigi Meiriraktagi (Poetry)
• **Thangjam Ibopishak Singh**	1997	Bhut Amasung Maikhum (Poetry)
• **Krisham Priyokumar**	1998	Nongdi Tarak-Khidare (Short Stories)
• **Sagolsem Lanchenba Meitei**	1999	Hi Nang bu-Hondeda (Poetry)
• **L. Premchand Singh**	2000	Eemagi Phanek Machet (Short Stories)
• **Ningombam Sunita**	2001	Khongji Makhal (Short Stories)
• **Rajkumar Bhubonsana**	2002	Mei Mamgera Budhi Mamgera (Poetry)
• **Sudhir Naoroibam**	2003	Leiyee Khara Punsi Khara (Short Stories)
• **Birendrajit Naorem**	2004	Lanthengndriba Lanmee (Poetry)
• **M. Nabakishore Singh**	2005	Pangal Shambu Eishe Adom geeni (Short Stories)
• **Saratchand Thiyam**	2006	Noongshibi Gris
• **B.N. Maisanamba**	2007	Imasi Nurabee (Novel)
• **A.O. Memchoubi**	2008	Idu Nidthoo (Poetry)
• **Raghu Leishangthem**	2009	Khungangi Chithi (Poetry)
• **M. Borkanya**	2010	Leikangla (Novel)
• **Kshetri Bira**	2011	Nangabu Dagaibada (Novel)
• **Jodha C. Sansam**	2012	Mathou Kanba DNA (Novel)
• **Makhonmani Mongasaba**	2013	Chinglon Amadagi Amada (Travelogues)
• **Naorem Bidyasagar Singh**	2014	Khung-gang Amasung Refugee (Poetry)
• **Kshetri Rajen**	2015	Ahingna Yekshilliba Mang (Poetry)
• **Moirangthem Rajen**	2016	Cheptharaba Eshing Pun (Short Stories)
• **Rajen Taijamba**	2017	Chahi Taret Khuntakpa (Play)
• **Budhichandra Heisnamba**	2018	Ngamkheigee Wangmada (Short Stories)
• **R.K. Sanahanbi Chanu**	2019	Jhawaishinggi Thawai (Play)

(No Awards has given in 1975 and 1980)

Sangeet Natak Akademi Awards/Fellowships

- Amubi Singh 1956
- H Atomba Singh 1958
- T Amudon Sharma 1961
- Ph Atombapu Sharma 1963
- Bipin Singh 1965
- Th. Chaoba Singh 1969
- Ksh. Tombi Devi 1972
- L Koireng Singh 1973
- L Ibemhal Devi 1974
- Rajani Maibi 1975
- Ibungohal Singh 1976
- Nayana Jhaveri 1977
- Th. Kunjakishor 1978
- S Kalidamon 1979
- Smt. Thouranishabi Devi 1980
- RK Priyogopalsana 1980
- K Ibomcha Sharma 1981
- I Rajanidhi Singh 1981
- L Tombi Devi 1982
- G Gourakishor Sharma 1983
- RK Singhajit Singh 1984
- Kh. Lokeshor Sharma 1985
- H Kanbailal 1985
- Th. Tarunkumar & Ratan Thiyam 1987
- G Ibopishak Sharma 1988
- Y Gambhini Devi 1988
- Th. Babu Singh 1990
- H Sabitri Devi 1991
- S Devabrata 1992
- H Nganbi Devi 1993
- S Thanil Singh & T Nodia 1994
- S Thanin 1995
- Darshana Jhaveri 1996
- R.K. Bhogen 1997
- Samanduram Tondon Devi 1997
- Y. Ranjana Devi 1997
- N. Madhabi Devi 1998
- Sorokhaibam Naran Singh 1999-2000
- L. Lakpati Singh 2001
- K. Onjbi Leipaklotpi Devi 2002
- T. Suryamukhi Devi 2003
- Kalavati Devi 2003
- L. Birendra Kumar Singh 2003
- Yumnam Rajendra Singh 2007
- Brinda Sabi Devi 2007
- N. Ibobi Singh 2008
- L. Ibohalmacha Singh 2009
- L. Bino Devi 2009
- Priti Patel 2011
- Ratan Thiyam 2012
- LN Oinam Ongbi Dhoni Devi 2017

Padma Awards

Recipient	*Year*	*Field*
• Atombapu Sharma	—	Literature
• Major Ralengnao Kathing	1957	Public Affairs
• Maisnam Amubi Singh	1970	Arts
• Ch. Kalachand Shastri	1971	Literature and Education
• T.A. Mudon Sharma	1972	Dance
• G.C. Tongbra	1975	Literature
• Smt. Lhingioneng Gangte	1975	Social Service
• M.K. Binodini Devi	1976	Literature and Education
• Shri L. Damu Singh	1983	Sports
• Dharamchand Patni	1984	Social Work
• A. Hinaketan Singh	1985	Literature
• Th. Haridas	1985	Social Service
• N. Khelchandra Ongjam	1987	Literature
• Ratan Thiyam	1989	Drama
• G. Surchand Sharma	1990	Literature & Social Service
• M. Kirti Singh	1992	Literature & Social Service
• Shri K. Ibomcha Sharma	1998	Arts
• R.K. Jhalajit Singh	1999	Literature

Recipient	Year	Field
• E. Nilakanta Singh	2000	Literature
• Shri L. Nabakishore Singh	2001	Herbal Medicine
• Smt. K.O. Thouranisabi Devi	2003	Arts
• Smt. Gurumayum Devi	2004	Sports
• Shri Heisnam Kanhailal	2004	Arts
• Shri Sougaijam Thanil Singh	2005	Arts
• Smt Y. Gambhini Devi	2005	Arts
• Aribam Shyam Sharma	2006	Arts
• Mangte C. Mary Kom	2006	Sports
• T. Babu Singh & Neelmani Devi	2007	Arts
• Sabitri Heisnam	2008	Arts
• Gurumayum Gourakishor Sharma	2009	Arts
• Haobam Angbi Naganbi Devi	2010	Arts
• Raj Kumar Achauba Singh	2010	Arts
• Aekpam Tom Muti	2010	Social Science
• N.I. Devi	2012	Arts
• M.C. Merrycom & N. Dingko Singh	2013	Sports
• Elam Endira Devi	2014	Arts
• Dr. Waikhom Gojen Meeitei	2014	Literature & Education
• Dr. S. Bimola Kumari Devi	2015	Medicine
• Heisnam Kanhailala	2016	Arts
• Laishram Birendra Kumar	2017	Art-Music
• Wareppa Naba Nil	2017	Art-Theatre
• Saikhom Mirabai Chanu	2018	Sports
• L. Subadani Devi	2018	Weavine-Art
• Bombayla Devi Laishram	2019	Sports

NATIONAL AWARDEES FOR FILMS FROM MANIPUR

Film	Year	Award	Director
• Matamgi Manipur	1972	President's Medal	Debkumar Bose
• Saphabee	1976	Best Regional Film	Aribam Shyam Sharma
• Khutthang Lamjel	1980	Best Regional Film	—
• Sanakeithel	1984	Best Regional Film	M.A. Singh
• The Deer of Manipur	1990	Best Environment/ Conservation/ Preservation Film	Aribam Shyam Sharma
• Ishanou	1991	Best Regional Film	Aribam Shyam Sharma
• Indigenous Games of Manipur	1991	Best Exploration/ Adventure Film	Aribam Shyam Sharma
• Meitei Pung	1992	Special Jury Award	Aribam Shyam Sharma
• Sambal Wangma	1993	Best Regional Film	K. Ibohal Sharma
• Orchids of Manipur	1994	Best Environment/ conservation/preser-vation Film	Aribam Shyam Sharma
• Moyophygee Macha	1995	Best Regional Film	Oken Amakcham
• Sanabi	1996	Best Regional Film	Aribam Shyam Sharma
• Yellhou Jagoi	1996	Best Anthropological and Enthnographical Film	Aribam Shyam Sharma
• Chatledo Eidi	2001	Best Regional Film	Makhonmani Mongsaba
• AFSPA 1958	2008	Best Non-Feature Film	Haobam Paban Kumar
• Phijigee Mani	2011	Best Regional Film	Oinam Gautam
• Loktak Lairembee	2017	Best Film on Environment	Haobam Paban Kumar

Arjuna Awards from Manipur

Year	Sports	Winners
• 1990	Weightlifting	N. Kunjarani Devi
• 1998	Boxing	Shri Ng. Dingko Singh
• 2000	Hockey	Ms. Tingonleima Chanu
	Weightlifting	Ms. Sanamacha Chanu Thingbaijam
• 2003	Boxing	M.C. Mary Kom
	Hockey	Suraj Lata Devi
• 2004	Judo	Angom Anita Chanu
• 2007	Judo	Tombi Devi
• 2008	Boxing	L. Sarita Devi
• 2011	Boxing	Suranjoy Singh
• 2011	Wushu	Sandhya Rani
• 2012	Archery	L. Bombayla Devi
• 2012	Weightlifting	Ng. Sonia Chanu
• 2012	Wushu	M. Bimoljit Singh
• 2014	Weightlifting	Y. Renubala Chanu
• 2015	Wushu	Y. Sanathoi Devi
• 2017	Football	Oinam Bembem Devi
• 2017	Boxing	L. Devendro Singh
• 2019	Hockey	Chinglensana Singh Kangujam

Rajiv Gandhi Khel Ratna Award

Year	Sports	Winners
• 1996	Weightlifting	N. Kunjarani Devi
• 2008-09	Boxing	M.C. Mary Kom
• 2018	Weightlifting	Mirabai Chanu

BOOKS & AUTHORS

Books	Authors
• Religion and Culture of Manipur	Dr M Kriti
• Queen Empress Vs Tikendrajit	John Parratt & Saroj Parrat
• My Sister	Saratchand Thiyam
• My Song a Mask	BS Rajkumar
• Metamorphosis of a Puppy	Yumlembam lbomcha
• Thisham	Mr KK Hugh
• Ithak Ipom	Nibir Shastri
• Ima	RK Shitaljit
• Langoi Shagol Thaba	Longjam Parshuram
• Numit Kappa	O Bhogeshor
• Laman	H Guno Singh
• Imagee Phanek Machet	L Prremachand
• Jahera	H Angahal Singh
• Leipareng	Dr Komol
• Elisha Amagi Mahao	N Kungamohon
• Khudol	H Guno Singh
• Labanga Lata	Kh. Chaoba
• Khamba Thoibi Sheireng	Hijam Angahal
• Madhabi	Dr Komol Singh
• My Experience in Manipur	Sir James Johnstone
• Geography of Manipur	S.A. Ansari

Books	Authors
• History of Manipur	J Ray
• The History of Manipur	W Ibohal Singh
• Introduction to Manipur	L Ibungobal Singh
• Manipur and Mainstream	N Tombi Singh
• History of Modern Manipur	Lal Dena
• Social Change of Manipur	BK Ahluwalia and Shashi Ahluwalia
• Manipur Maid of the Mountains	R Constantine
• Manipur and Naga Hills	Sir James Johnstone
• The Religion of Manipur	Saroj Nalini Parratt
• My three years in Manipur	Mrs Grim Woods
• Valley of Manipur	Mc Oulloh
• People of Manipur	Grim Woods
• The Meiteis	TC Hudson
• Gazetteer of Manipur	EW Dun
• Bor Shahep Ongbi Sanatombi	MK Binodini
• A Short History of Manipur	RK Jhalajit
• Art of Manipur	Nilima Roy
• Cheitharol Kumbaba	Llbungohal & N. Khelchandra
• Constraints in Development of Manipur	C. Joshua Thomas, R. Gopalakrishnan and R.K. Ranjan Singh
• Development Priorities in North-East India	Bimal J. Deb
• Dimension of Rural Development in North-East India	B. Datta Ray and Gurudas Das
• Ethnicity in Manipur : Experiences, Issues and Perspectives	Lucy Zehol
• Fables and Folk Tales of Manipur	G.K. Ghosh; Shukla Ghosh
• Folk Culture of Manipur	M.K. Singh
• Fragments of Manipuri Culture	E. Nilakanta Singh
• History, Religion and Culture of North East India	T. Raatan
• History of Manipur	Gangmumei Kabui
• History of Manipur	Jyotirmoy Roy
• Loktak Lake : Manipur (Ramsar Sites of India)	H. Tombi Singh
• Manipur	L.R. Singh
• Manipur : Geography and Regional Development	Vedaja Sanjenbam
• Manipur : Religion, Culture and Society	Chander Sheikhar Panchani

Books	*Authors*
• Manipur : The Jewel of India	S.C. Joshi
• Manipur : A Tourist Paradise	E. Ishwarjit Singh
• Manipur A British Anthology (I, II), 2005	Naorem Sanajaoba
• Manipur : The Glorious Past	A.K. Sharma
• Manipur: Tribal Demography and Socio-economic Development	S.A. Ansari
• Manipur : Culture and Politics	Bimal J. Dev
• Manipur : Past and Present: The Heritage and Ordeals of A Civilization (Vol. 1), 1998 (Vol. II, III, IV), 2005	Naorem Sanajaoba
• Manipur Treaties (Vol. 1)	Naorem Sanajaoba
• Manipuri Dance	E. Nilakanta Singh
• Mei Mamgera Budhi Mamgera	R.K. Bhubonsana
• Merger of Manipur	H. Bhuban Singh
• Mao : The Naga Tribe of Manipur	Lorho Mary Maheo
• Nongdi Tarak-Khidare	Keisham Priyokumar Singh
• Rising Manipur Including Other North-Eastern States	M. Horam
• Shaktam Macha Machasing	Dr N. Tombi
• Social Movements in Manipur: 1917-1951	N. Joykumar Singh
• Some Aspects of The Geography of Manipur	S.A. Ansari
• The Boundaries of Manipur	Dr. L. Chandramani Singh
• The Kukis of Manipur : A historical Analysis	T.S. Gangte
• Traditional Textiles of Manipur	Muttua Bahadur
• Tribal Agrarian System of Manipur	L. Chinzakham Ngaihte
• Tribal Land System of Manipur	P. Binodini Devi
• Valley Society of Manipur: A Cultural Frontier of Indian Civilization	R.K. Saha
• Egi Machu Khetnada	Landon Kabui

Census 2011

The Census of India 2011, is historic and epoch making being the second census of the twenty-first century. It reveals benchmark data on the state of abundant human resources available in the country, their demography, culture and economic structure at a juncture, which marks a centennial and millenial transition.

Census of India comprises of Population, Population-Density, Sex Ratio and Literacy. One of the important indices of population concentration in census is the density of population which is the number of persons per square kilometre. Sex ratio is the number of females per thousand males while a person aged seven, and above, who can both read and write with understanding in any language, is treated as literate.

The districts of the states play an important role in census. As an administrative unit, district assumes a lot of significance in the context of decentralized planning and implementation of various plans and programmes. Therefore, deciding on an appropriate size of a district in terms of population and geographical area is a vital and essential element in creating an effective administrative set up.

Census 2011 reveals that Tamenglong is the least populous district of Manipur while the Imphal West is the most literate district. Imphal West tops in the category of sex ratio, whereas child population (0-6) years is higher in Thoubal than any other district. Given below are the tables showing population, density, literacy rate etc. district wise for the entire state of Manipur.

POPULATION

Manipur : 2,855,794 (***Males :*** 1,438,586 ***Females :*** 1,417,208)

S.No.	*District*	*Population*	*Male*	*Female*
1	Senapati	479,148	247,323	231,825
2	Tamenglong	1,40,651	72,371	68,280
3	Churachandpur	2,74,143	1,38,820	1,35,323
4	Bishnupur	2,37,399	1,18,782	1,18,617
5	Thoubal	4,22,168	2,10,845	2,11,323
6	Imphal West	5,17,992	2,55,054	2,62,938
7	Imphal East	4,56,113	2,26,094	2,30,019
8	Ukhrul	1,83,998	94,718	89,280
9	Chandel	1,44,182	74,579	69,603

DECADAL GROWTH RATE

Manipur (1991-2001) : 24.86%, (2001-2011) : 24.50%

S.No.	District	1991-2001	2001-2011
1	Senapati	36.09	68.9
2	Tamenglong	29.23	26.1
3	Churachandpur	29.36	20.3
4	Bishnupur	15.27	13.9
5	Thoubal	23.87	15.9
6	Imphal West	16.70	16.6
7	Imphal East	19.49	15.5
8	Ukhrul	28.83	30.7
9	Chandel	66.62	21.9

SEX RATIO

Manipur (2001) : 978, (2011) : 985

Sex Ratio and Rate of Change in the Sex Ratio in India and Manipur(1901-2011)

Year	Sex Ratio		Rate of Change in PC	
	India	Manipur	India	Manipur
1901	972	1037		
1911	964	1029	–0.82	–0.77
1921	955	1041	–0.93	–0.17
1931	950	1065	–0.52	+2.31
1941	945	1055	–0.53	–0.94
1951	946	1036	+0.11	–1.80
1961	941	1015	–0.53	–2.03
1971	930	980	–1.17	–3.45
1981	934	971	+0.43	–0.92
1991	927	958	–0.75	–1.34
2001	933	978	+0.64	+2.04
2011	943	985	+0.74	+0.91

District Wise Sex Ratio in Manipur (1971-2011)

S.No.	District	1971	1981	1991	2001	2011
1	Senapati	950	929	942	928	937
2	Tamenglong	1016	975	935	922	943
3	Churachandpur	976	929	931	993	975
4	Bishnupur	–	–	984	1004	999
5	Thoubal	–	–	980	998	1002
6	Imphal West	–	–	979	1007	1031
7	Imphal East	–	–	966	992	1017
8	Ukhrul	969	917	884	920	943
9	Chandel	975	935	913	986	933
	State	980	971	958	978	985

DENSITY

Manipur(2001) : 97; (2011) : 128

S.No.	District	2001	2011
1	Senapati	48	146
2	Tamenglong	25	32
3	Churachandpur	50	60
4	Bishnupur	420	479
5	Thoubal	708	821
6	Imphal West	856	998
7	Imphal East	557	643
8	Ukhrul	31	40
9	Chandel	36	44

CHILD POPULATION (0–6 YEARS)

Manipur : 3,38,254 (Males : 1,74,700; Females : 1,63,554)

S.No.	District	Total	Male	Female
1	Senapati	26,232	13,679	12,553
2	Tamenglong	19,307	10,072	9,235
3	Churachandpur	37,445	19,227	18,218
4	Bishnupur	31,303	16,192	15,111
5	Thoubal	60,556	31,294	29,262
6	Imphal West	61,875	31,747	30,128
7	Imphal East	59,936	30,851	29,085
8	Ukhrul	24,413	12,693	11,720
9	Chandel	17,187	8,945	8,242

LITERACY

Manipur : 19,08,476 (Males : 10,39,858; Females : 8,68,618)

S.No.	District	Total	Male	Female
1	Senapati	2,64,477	1,48,012	1,16,465
2	Tamenglong	85,006	47,403	37,603
3	Churachandpur	1,95,935	1,04,013	91,922
4	Chandel	90,302	51,053	39,249
5	Ukhrul	1,29,829	70,148	59,631
6	Imphal (E)	3,24,664	1,73,314	1,51,350
7	Imphal (W)	3,92,626	2,05,985	1,86,641
8	Bishnupur	1,56,333	87,313	69,020
9	Thoubal	2,69,304	1,52,617	1,16,687

LITERACY RATE

Manipur (2001)	:	70.50	Manipur (2011)	:	76.94
Males	:	80.30	Males	:	83.58
Females	:	60.50	Females	:	70.26

S.No.	District	2001			2011		
		Total	Male	Female	Total	Male	Female
1	Senapati	59.8	67.9	51.2	63.60	69.21	57.67
2	Tamenglong	59.2	68.7	49.0	70.05	76.09	63.69
3	Churachandpur	70.6	77.7	63.1	82.78	86.97	78.50
4	Bishnupur	67.6	79.6	55.7	75.85	85.11	66.68
5	Thoubal	66.4	80.4	52.5	74.47	85.00	64.09
6	Imphal West	80.2	89.2	71.3	86.08	92.24	80.17
7	Imphal East	75.4	85.5	65.3	81.95	88.77	75.32
8	Ukhrul	73.1	80.1	65.4	81.35	85.52	76.95
9	Chandel	56.2	64.3	48.0	71.11	77.78	63.96

NUMBER OF SC AND ST OF MANIPUR BY SEX

Year	Scheduled Castes	Scheduled Tribes	% to total state population	
			S.C.	S.T.
1961	13,376	2,49,049	1.71	31.93
1971	16,376	3,34,466	1.53	31.18
1981	17,753	3,87,977	1.25	27.30
1991	37,105	6,32,173	2.02	34.41
2001	60,037	7,41,141	2.77	34.20
2011	97,328	11,67,422	3.41	40.88

RURAL AND URBAN POPULATION

According to 2011, 70.79% of the total population are found in rural areas while 29.21% are settled in the urban areas. Similar pattern are observed at the regional level also. However, the concentration of population in the rural areas is much higher in the hill region (92.70%) as compared to the valley region (54.40%). The per centage of urban population to the District population is found to be highest in Imphal West Districts (62.33%) among the Valley Districts and in Ukhrul District (14.78%) among the Hill Districts. And the least concentration of urban population is found in Senapati District with only 1.56% and the second least in Churachandpur District with 6.70%.

RURAL AND URBAN POPULATION–2011

Region/District/	Population			Percentage of total population	
State	Rural	Urban	Total	Rural	Urban
1	2	3	4	5	6
A. HILL	**1,132,892**	**89,230**	**1,222,122**	**92.70**	**7.30**
Senapati	471,672	7,476	479,148	98.44	1.56
Tamenglong	121,288	19,363	140,6510	86.23	13.77
Churachandpur	255,786	18,357	274,143	93.30	6.70
Chandel	127,335	16,847	144,182	88.32	11.68
Ukhrul	156,811	27,187	183,998	85.22	14.78
B. VALLEY	**888,748**	**744,924**	**1633,672**	**54.40**	**45.60**
Imphal East	272,906	183,207	456,113	59.83	40.17
Imphal West	195,113	322,879	517,992	37.67	62.33
Bishnupur	149,894	87,505	237,399	63.14	36.86
Thoubal	270,835	151,333	422,168	64.15	36.02
Manipur	**20,21,640**	**834,154**	**2,855,794**	**70.79**	**29.21**

MANIPUR

MULTIPLE CHOICE QUESTIONS

1. What is the total area of Manipur?
A. 22327 sq. km.
B. 22223 sq. km.
C. 22732 sq. km.
D. 22237 sq. km.

2. In which year Manipur became the twentieth state of the Indian Union?
A. 1970
B. 1971
C. 1972
D. 1973

3. In Manipur Jadonang was hanged in August, 1931. Who was Jadonang?
A. A great Naga leader
B. A great Zome leader
C. A great Zeliangrong leader
D. A great Meitei leader

4. In which year revered king Pakhangba ascended the throne?
A. 30 A.D.
B. 31 A.D.
C. 32 A.D.
D. 33 A.D.

5. When was the Manipur Constitution Act passed?
A. 1947
B. 1948
C. 1949
D. 1950

6. In which year Nara Singha became the King of Manipur?
A. 1832
B. 1840
C. 1844
D. 1848

7. How many states touch the boundary of Manipur?
A. 3
B. 4
C. 5
D. 6

8. In which year was the Battle of Khongjom fought?
A. 1885
B. 1887
C. 1890
D. 1891

9. In which year did Manipur become a Union Territory?
A. 1950
B. 1955
C. 1956
D. 1960

10. When was Shillong Accord signed?
A. 15 Oct., 1949
B. 20 Sep., 1950
C. 25 Nov., 1952
D. 15 Aug., 1957

---

1. A **2.** C **3.** C **4.** D **5.** A **6.** C **7.** A **8.** D **9.** C **10.** A

11. Who was the last King of Manipur?
A. Maharaja Gambhir Singh B. Maharaja Tikendrajit Singh
C. Maharaja Ranjit Singh D. Maharaja Purandar Singh

12. During the first world war, which King ruled over in Manipur?
A. Maharaja Nara Singha B. Maharaja Garibniwaz
C. Maharaja Chandrakirti Singh D. Maharaja Koineng Singh

13. During the reign of which King of Kangleipak was the title ''Manipur'' named after it?
A. Maharaja Churachand Singh
B. Maharaja Garibniwaz
C. Maharaja Bhagyachandra
D. Maharaja Chandrakirti Singh

14. What is the Capital of Manipur?
A. Imphal B. Bishnupur
C. Churachandpur D. Thoubal

15. What is the total number of districts in Manipur?
A. Eight B. Sixteen
C. Ten D. Twelve

16. What is the total population of Manipur as per the 2011 census?
A. 30,48,756 B. 28,55,794
C. 32,27,309 D. 22,18,960

17. When was the census started in Manipur?
A. 1750 B. 1752
C. 1757 D. 1760

18. When did Manipur come under the British rule?
A. 12 April, 1891 B. 12 March, 1890
C. 10 May, 1885 D. 5 June, 1860

19. How many Autonomous District Councils are there in Manipur?
A. Five B. Six
C. Seven D. Eight

20. How many Legislative Assembly Constituencies are there in Manipur?
A. 50 B. 60
C. 70 D. 75

---

11. A **12.** C **13.** B **14.** A **15.** B **16.** B **17.** C **18.** A **19.** B **20.** B

21. Which is the biggest river in Manipur?
A. Iril
B. Sekmai
C. Barrak
D. Nambul

22. Which one of the following is not a physical division of Manipur?
A. Churachandpur
B. Manipur Hills
C. Manipur Valley
D. Jiribam Plains

23. How many MLAs are elected from the Hill Districts to the Manipur Legislative Assembly?
A. 20
B. 25
C. 30
D. 35

24. In Manipur Assembly how many seats are reserved for Scheduled Tribes?
A. 15
B. 19
C. 25
D. 30

25. On what date Martyr's Day is observed in Manipur?
A. 10th August
B. 13th August
C. 15th August
D. 18th August

26. In which District Khangkhui Caves are located?
A. Chandel
B. Ukhrul
C. Senapati
D. Tamenglong

27. Which is the first Manipuri colour feature film?
A. Imagee Ningthem
B. Brojendrogi Luhongba
C. Langlen Thadai
D. Matamgi Manipur

28. Which is the first Manipuri feature film?
A. Ishanou
B. Khonjel
C. Saphabee
D. Matamgi Manipur

29. Who is the first Manipuri to win the Arjuna Award?
A. Dingko Singh
B. N. Kunjarani Devi
C. M.C. Mary Kom
D. Suraj Lata Devi

30. Who is the first Manipuri to win the Sahitya Academy Award?
A. Pacha Meeitei
B. N. Kunjamohan Singh
C. L. Samarendra Singh
D. A. Minaketan Singh

---

21. C **22.** A **23.** A **24.** B **25.** B **26.** B **27.** C **28.** D **29.** B **30.** A

31. Who was the first woman MLA (Member of Legislative Assembly)?
A. Kim Gangte B. W. Leima Devi
C. Hangmila Shaija D. None of these

32. Who was the first Chief Minister of Manipur State?
A. M. Kaireng Singh B. L. Thambou Singh
C. M.K. Priyobrata Singh D. R.K. Dorendra Singh

33. Who was the first Lok Sabha member from the Inner Parliamentary Constituency of Manipur?
A. L. Jugeswar Singh B. L. Achaw Singh
C. S. Tombi Singh D. M. Meghachandra

34. Who was the first Lok Sabha member from the outer Parliamentary Constituency of Manipur?
A. Rungsung Suisa B. Rishang Keishing
C. Paokai Haokip D. Yangmaso Shaiza

35. Heikru Hitongba festival was introduced in Manipur in :
A. 1778 B. 1775
C. 1779 D. 1772

36. Who was the first Governor of Manipur?
A. L.P. Singh B. S.M.H. Burney
C. K.V. Krishna Rao D. B.K. Nehru

37. Who was the first Rajya Sabha M.P. from Manipur?
A. Ng. Tompok Singh B. L. Lalit Madhob Sharma
C. S. Krishnamohan Singh D. Salam Tombi Singh

38. How many members represent Manipur in the Rajya Sabha?
A. 1 B. 2
C. 3 D. 4

39. How many members represent Manipur in the Lok Sabha?
A. 2 B. 4
C. 5 D. 7

40. In which year Manipur became a full fledged state?
A. 1970 B. 1972
C. 1973 D. 1974

---

31. C **32.** C **33.** A **34.** B **35.** C **36.** D **37.** A **38.** A **39.** A **40.** B

41. When did the Gauhati High Court come into existence in Manipur?
A. 21-1-1972 B. 21-4-1970
C. 21-4-1971 D. 21-4-1973

42. In which of the following rivers does the Imphal river fall?
A. The Iril river B. The Loktak lake
C. The Brahmaputra D. The Chindwin river

43. In which year Imphal District was divided?
A. 1995 B. 1996
C. 1997 D. 1998

44. When was the "Khongjom War" fought in Manipur?
A. 23-7-1891 B. 23-6-1891
C. 23-4-1891 D. 16-9-1890

45. Who is the first olympian from Manipur?
A. P. Nilkamal Singh B. N. Kunjarani Devi
C. H.L. Tangkhul D. Thoiba Singh

46. 'Nongyeen' was declared as the State Bird of Manipur in the year :
A. 1986 B. 1987
C. 1988 D. 1989

47. The first Legislative Assembly was inaugurated in Manipur in :
A. 1961 B. 1962
C. 1963 D. 1964

48. In which lake the Sendra island is situated?
A. Loukai lake B. Waithou lake
C. Ikop lake D. Loktak lake

49. Which is the 'State Bird' of Manipur?
A. Tragopan B. Ashangba
C. Nongyeen D. Langmeidon

50. Who is the first sports person from Manipur to win a gold medal in the Asian Games?
A. N. Kunjarani Devi
B. Suraj Lata Devi
C. M.C. Mary Kom
D. Dingko Singh

---

41. A **42.** D **43.** C **44.** C **45.** A **46.** D **47.** C **48.** D **49.** C **50.** D

51. In which year Manipuri language was included in the 8th schedule of the Indian Constitution?
A. 1990 B. 1991 C. 1992 D. 1993

52. Pamheiba was the most powerful kings of Manipur in whose reign the state reached the pinnacle as a powerful state. His original name was—
A. Madhuchandra B. Churachand Singh
C. Chandrakirti D. Garibniwaz

53. When did Doordarshan start in Manipur?
A. 30 April, 1990 B. 30 April, 1991
C. 30 April, 1992 D. 30 April, 1993

54. What is the percentage of land under the cultivation in Manipur to its area?
A. Nearly 10% B. Narly 20%
C. Nearly 30% D. Nearly 40%

55. Who is the poet of ''Dustbin Amagi Warri''?
A. R. Constantine B. T.C. Hudson
C. T. Ibopishak Singh D. Vedaja Sanjenbam

56. How many recognised Tribal communities are in Manipur?
A. 30 B. 32 C. 34 D. 36

57. How many years Manipur remained as a part state and Union Territory?
A. Twenty B. Twenty one
C. Twenty two D. Twenty four

58. During the reign of which King in Manipur the first Telegraph line and Telegraph office were established?
A. Maharaja Chandrakirti in 1886
B. Maharaja Madhuchandra in 1801
C. Maharaja Yumjaotaba in 1820
D. Maharaja Churachand Singh in 1891

59. Which period was known as the ''Dark Period'' in Manipur?
A. 1730 A.D. to 1750 A.D. B. 1755 A.D. to 1826 A.D.
C. 1650 A.D. to 1726 A.D. D. 1820 A.D. to 1850 A.D.

60. ''Manipur is the Jewel of India and Switzerland of the East''. Who said this quotation?
A. Jawaharlal Nehru B. Mahatma Gandhi
C. Subhash Chandra Bose D. M. Kaireng Singh

---

51. C **52.** D **53.** C **54.** A **55.** C **56.** B **57.** C **58.** A **59.** B **60.** A

61. Who introduced Polo in Manipur?
A. Thayanthaba
B. Ebudhou Marjing
C. Garibniwaj
D. Koiremba

62. Who introduced ''Boat Race'' in Manipur?
A. Thangbi Lanthabu
B. Keiphaba Yanglon
C. Ninthou Punshiba
D. Gambhir Singha

63. When did Hindu Priest Santidash Goshai come to Manipur?
A. 1550 A.D. B. 1600 A.D.
C. 1760 A.D. D. 1716 A.D.

64. When was Manipur State Film Festival started?
A. 1982 B. 1983
C. 1984 D. 1985

65. What is the state language of Manipur?
A. Manipuri B. English
C. Hindi D. None of these

66. In Manipuri week days 'Nongmaijing' is known as :
A. Monday B. Sunday
C. Tuesday D. Wednesday

67. In which year was 'Meitei Chanu' the first journal of Manipur published?
A. 1920 B. 1922
C. 1924 D. 1926

68. The number of Jila Parishads in Manipur is :
A. 3 B. 4
C. 5 D. 6

69. 'Chon Festival' is celebrated by which tribe of Manipur?
A. Aimol B. Kabui Naga
C. Thadou D. Kuki

70. How many alphabets were there in the original Meitei language?
A. 20 B. 22
C. 25 D. 27

---

61. B **62.** C **63.** D **64.** C **65.** A **66.** B **67.** B **68.** B **69.** C **70.** D

71. When did Doordarshan's Metro Channel (DD2) start in Manipur?
A. December 23, 1995 B. December 23, 1990
C. December 23, 1991 D. December 23, 1992

72. The historic Kangla Fort Complex was formally handed back to the people of Manipur in the presence of the former Prime Minister Manmohan Singh on :
A. 20th November, 2004 B. 20th November, 2005
C. 20th November, 2006 D. 22nd November, 2006

73. When was the first ''Nupi Lal'' happened in Manipur?
A. 1904 A.D. B. 1905 A.D.
C. 1906 A.D. D. 1907 A.D.

74. In which district of Manipur can we find ''DZUKU LILY''?
A. Imphal East B. Chandel
C. Senapati D. Thoubal

75. Which Manipuri scholar was called the ''Agyestha of the East'' by Smiti Kumar Chatterjee?
A. Shyam Sharma B. E. Nilakanta Singh
C. C. Joshua Thomas D. Atombapu Sharma

76. The founder of the Praja Sameleni was :
A. Hijam Irabat Singh B. Lalita Madhop
C. Elangbam Tompok D. Aaiga Bankabihari

77. Who is the author of the book 'Labangalata'?
A. Lucy Zehol B. Khwairakpam Chaoba
C. M.K. Singh D. E.W. Dun

78. The Sangai Deer is found at which National Park/wild life sanctuary in Manipur?
A. Sirohi B. Keilam
C. Keibul Lamjao D. Yaingangpokpi Lakchao

79. Tharon caves are located in which district of Manipur?
A. Chandel B. Thoubal
C. Tamenglong D. Senapati

80. What is the state tree of Manipur?
A. Teak B. Pine
C. Parkia Javanica D. Uningthou

---

71. A **72.** A **73.** A **74.** C **75.** D **76.** A **77.** B **78.** C **79.** C **80.** D

81. Who become the first woman minister in Manipur?
A. R. Apabi Devi B. Kh. Thoibi Devi
C. Kim Gangte D. Khaidem Sakhi Devi

82. The state of Manipur lies between .... and .... east Longitude.
A. 80.20° and 84.35° B. 92.58° and 94.45°
C. 75.10° and 60.20° D. 96.20° and 99.13°

83. In which year Manipur Olympic Association was formed?
A. 1947 B. 1948
C. 1949 D. 1950

84. Who was the founder President of the Manipur Olympic Association?
A. Churachand Singh B. R.K. Madhuryajit Singh
C. Kalachandra D. Debendra Singh

85. Who was the founder of the ''Ningthouja Dynasty'' in Manipur?
A. Nongdalairen Pakhangba B. Atom Yairemba
C. Keiphaba Yanglon D. Nongchup Lamgaingamba

86. Who was the King of Manipur when the Burmese invaded in the year of 1819?
A. King Loyumba B. King Marjit Singh
C. King Gambhir Singh D. King Kiyamba Singh

87. Who was the first British Political Agent of Manipur?
A. George Gordon B. Grimwood
C. Captain William D. James Hednic

88. Who introduced ''Bell metal currency'' in Manipur?
A. Kyamba Maharaj B. Maramba Maharaj
C. Khagemba Maharaj D. Labanyachandra Maharaj

89. Porompat, Keirao Bitra and Sawombung are the sub-divisions of which district?
A. Churachandpur B. Chandel
C. Imphal West D. Imphal East

90. Who among the following was not the Chief-Minister of Manipur?
A. Md. Alimuddin B. P. Brojen Singh
C. M.K. Priyobratta D. Rishang Keishing

---

81. A **82.** B **83.** A **84.** B **85.** A **86.** B **87.** A **88.** C **89.** D **90.** B

91. Who introduced 'Vaishnavism' as a state Religion?

A. King Chingthangkhomba B. King Koiremba
C. King Bhagyachandra D. King Bharatsai

92. Who may be given the title of the ''First Modern Political Leader of Manipur?

A. Hijam Irabat Singh B. L. Jugeswar Singh
C. Paokai Haokip D. Ng. Tompok Singh

93. The first English Journal of Manipur 'Meitei Leirang' was published in :

A. 1965 B. 1969
C. 1972 D. 1975

94. Which is the first Health Journal of Manipur?

A. Chingtam B. Sanaleibak
C. Meeyam D. Meitei Maiba

95. Who was the first speaker of Manipur Legislative Assembly?

A. T.C. Tiankham B. Sibo Larho
C. M. Koireng Singh D. Tombi Singh

96. What is the literacy rate of Manipur as per the 2011 census?

A. 65.36 per cent B. 72.16 per cent
C. 76.94 per cent D. 75.24 per cent

97. What is the density of population in Manipur as per the 2011 census?

A. 128 B. 110
C. 132 D. 120

98. Who is the first Manipuri girl to become Miss East India?

A. Aparna Jhaveri B. Bonnie Gurumayum
C. Gayatri Heisnam D. Priyanka Kokila

99. The number of Universities in Manipur is :

A. 2 B. 3
C. 4 D 5

100. Manipur University was established in :

A. 1977 B. 1978
C. 1979 D. 1980

---

91. C **92.** A **93.** B **94.** D **95.** A **96.** C **97.** A **98.** B **99.** A **100.** D

101. Board of Secondary Education, Manipur was established in :
A. 1972-73 B. 1974-75 C. 1976-77 D. 1978-79

102. Script of the Grand Prix award winning film 'Imagee Ningthem' is written by :
A. N. Kunjamohan B. M.K. Binodini
C. A.K. Paul D. L.R. Singh

103. 'Seven Years Devastation' (Chahi Taret Khuntakpa) covers the period from :
A. 1810 to 1816 B. 1819 to 1825
C. 1829 to 1835 D. 1827 to 1833

104. When did the Manipur State Archieves set up?
A. 1980 B. 1982 C. 1985 D. 1988

105. Who described Manipur as ''An oasis of comparative civilization amidst the Barbarians?''
A. James Hotten B. William Ban
C. Alfred Lyll D. George Linde

106. Who is known as Queen of Boxing in Manipur?
A. M.C. Meri Kom B. N. Kunjarani Devi
C. Suraj Lata Devi D. Brojeswari Devi

107. During the reign of which King of Manipur the ''Scout Movement'' was started in the state?
A. Maharaja Chalamba Singh
B. Maharaja Chura Chand Singh
C. Maharaja Bharatsai Singh
D. Maharaja Ching Thang Khomba Singh

108. What is the area of Kangla, the ancient palace of Manipur?
A. 240.56 acres B. 350.16 acres
C. 237.62 acres D. 290.48 acres

109. Who is the first chairman of Hill Area Committee?
A. P.K. Mohan B. P.C. Mathew
C. E.P. Moon Jan D. S.P. Henry

110. When was the first Community Development Block established in Manipur?
A. 1952 B. 1953 C. 1954 D. 1955

---

101. A **102.** B **103.** B **104.** B **105.** C **106.** A **107.** B **108.** C **109.** D **110.** A

111. Keilam Wildlife Sanctuary is located in which district?
A. Churachandpur B. Senapati
C. Thoubal D. Ukhrul

112. How many airports are there in Manipur?
A. 1 B. 2
C. 3 D. 4

113. Which is the first railway station of Manipur?
A. Dimapur Railway Station
B. Jiribam Railway Station
C. Toubal Railway Station
D. Karong Railway Station

114. Where is airport of Manipur located?
A. Churachandpur B. Tamenglong
C. Imphal D. Chandel

115. What is the 'State Game' of Manipur?
A. Thang Yannaba B. Mangjong
C. Lamjel D. Sagol Kangjei

116. In which year 'Manipur Hockey Association' was formed?
A. 1976 B. 1977
C. 1978 D. 1979

117. The author of the book 'Bir Tikendrajit Road' is :
A. T.C. Hudson B. Hijam Guno
C. Nilima Roy D. Lal Dena

118. Who is the first Manipuri to appear on postage stamp?
A. Laishram Memma B. Jugeswori Devi
C. Rani Gaidenlilu D. Rashi Devi

119. Who is the first person from Manipur to receive the 'Padmashree'?
A. N. Kunjarani Devi B. Irom Leikhendra
C. P. Neelkamal D. Atombapu Sharma

120. The number of Industrial Training Institutes in Manipur is :
A. Four B. Five
C. Six D. Eleven

---

111. A **112.** A **113.** B **114.** C **115.** D **116.** A **117.** B **118.** C **119.** D **120.** D

121. Manipur Handloom and Handicrafts Development Corporation was set-up in :
A. 1972 B. 1976
C. 1980 D. 1982

122. In which year was the Manipur State Museum established?
A. 1965 B. 1969
C. 1975 D. 1979

123. What is Manipuri Polo called :
A. Yubi Lakpi B. Khong Kangjei
C. Mukna Kangjei D. Sagol Kangjei

124. Who was the first Deputy Chief Minister of Manipur?
A. L. Jugeshwar Singh B. M. Koireng Singh
C. Irengbam Tompok Singh D. Yangmasho Shaiza

125. When was the 'Patriot Day'' observed at the first time in Manipur?
A. 1965 B. 1966
C. 1968 D. 1969

126. Which King introduced the system of 'Division of Labour'' in Manipur?
A. King Loyumba B. King Marjit Singh
C. King Gambhir Singh D. King Khagemba Singh

127. Who is the writer of the book ''Elisa Amagi Mahao''?
A. E. Nilakanta Singh
B. N. Kunja Mohan Singh
C. G.C. Tongbra
D. A. Minaketan Singh

128. When was the first ''District Library established in Manipur?
A. 1950 B. 1952
C. 1955 D. 1958

129. R.K. Chandrajit Singh is related to :
A. painting B. writing
C. music D. sport

130. In which district of Manipur the highest hill mount Tenipu is situated?
A. Senapati B. Imphal East
C. Thoubal D. Bishnupur

---

121. B **122.** B **123.** D **124.** C **125.** D **126.** A **127.** B **128.** D **129.** A **130.** A

131. The largest pineapple producer district of Manipur is :
A. Bishnupur B. Thoubal
C. Tamenglong D. Ukhrul

132. 'Manipur Film Society' was established in :
A. 1955 B. 1960
C. 1962 D. 1966

133. Which is the first Manipuri documentary film?
A. Maipak – the Son of Manipur
B. Meitei Pung
C. Chatldo Eidi
D. Yellhou Jagai

134. Who is the director of first Manipuri documentary film?
A. M.A. Singh B. Aribam Shyam Sharma
C. Devkumar Bose D. Oken Amakcham

135. The Number of National Highway passes through Manipur is :
A. 3 B. 4
C. 5 D. 6

136. When was the Jiribam Railway Station inaugurated?
A. 1990 B. 1982
C. 1987 D. 1992

137. The number of Post Offices (2011) in Manipur is :
A. 1200 B. 1394
C. 1060 D. 970

138. Which is the largest export-oriented agricultural product of Manipur?
A. Maize B. Rice
C. Cotton D. Wheat

139. Manipur State Kala Academy was established in :
A. 1965 B. 1970
C. 1972 D. 1975

140. What is the average height of Imphal valley above MSL (mean sea level)?
A. 790 metres B. 850 metres
C. 990 metres D. 1050 metres

---

131. B **132.** D **133.** A **134.** C **135.** A **136.** A **137.** B **138.** A **139.** C **140.** A

141. Who started the festival of Kang-Chingba (Ratha Yatra) in Manipur?
A. Maharaja Jai Singh B. Maharaja Madhuchandra
C. Maharaja Churachand Singh D. Maharaja Gambhir Singh

142. The Meeteis were converted into Hinduism during the reign of which king?
A. King Garibniwaz B. King Maramba
C. King Marjit D. King Kyamba

143. When was the last independent war of Manipur fought against British?
A. 20th March 1875 to 25th June 1875
B. 24th March 1891 to 27th April 1891
C. 15th January 1890 to 25th February 1890
D. 10th May 1879 to 27 July 1879

144. What is the serial number of Manipuri as it is listed in the Eight schedule to the constitution of India?
A. 9th B. 10th C. 11th D. 12th

145. The judges of Manipur High Court are appointed by :
A. The Chief Justice of India
B. The President of India
C. The Chief Minister of Manipur
D. The Governor of Manipur

146. The language spoken by the largest number of people in the Manipur is :
A. English B. Bengali C. Hindi D. Manipuri

147. What was the old name of Senapati district?
A. Manipur East B. Manipur West
C. Manipur North D. Manipur South

148. What was the old name of Chandel district?
A. Central District B. Manipur West
C. Manipur East D. Tengnoupal

149. The ornament, which is worn around the neck by the Manipuri women, is called :
A. Khonanakpi B. Khuji C. Khorau D. Kanberi

150. In which year Manipur was included on the Indian Railway Map?
A. 1989 B. 1990 C. 1991 D. 1992

---

141. D **142.** A **143.** B **144.** A **145.** B **146.** D **147.** C **148.** D **149.** A **150.** B

151. As per the 2011 census what is the sex ratio in Manipur?

A. 985 B. 980
C. 975 D. 995

152. Loktak Project was commissioned in :

A. 1983 B. 1984
C. 1985 D. 1986

153. In which district of Manipur Zoological Garden is located?

A. Tamenglong B. Imphal
C. Churachandpur D. Bishnupur

154. Manipur Agro-Industries Corporation was set-up in :

A. 1989 B. 1990
C. 1991 D. 1992

155. The last Lieutenant Governor of Manipur was :

A. J.M. Raina B. P.C. Mathew
C. D.R. Kohil D. Baleshwar Prasad

156. Which King introduced Kwak Tomba religious ceremony in Manipur?

A. Khuiyoi Tompok B. Keiphaba Yanglon
C. Khui Ningngomba D. Chingthang Lanthaba

157. During the reign of which King in Manipur the game Yubi Lakpi first played?

A. King Thawanthaba B. King Chingthangkhomba
C. King Lanthaba D. King Ayangba

158. In which district of Manipur Khagemba's old palace was situated?

A. Bishnupur B. Churachandpur
C. Chandel D. Ukhrul

159. Jhaveri sisters are famous for :

A. Odissi Dance B. Kathak
C. Manipuri Dance D. Bharat Natyam

160. Manipur Theological college is located at :

A. Thoubal B. Ukhrul
C. Imphal D. Chadel

---

151. A **152.** A **153.** B **154.** D **155.** C **156.** C **157.** A **158.** B **159.** C **160.** C

161. In Manipur INA Museum is located at :
A. Moirang B. Nambal
C. Kakching D. Lilong

162. Where is the state Museum of Manipur situated?
A. Chandel B. Senapati
C. Imphal D. Tamenglong

163. Who was Manipur's first MBBS Doctor?
A. Dr. Nanda Babu Roy B. Dr. P.K. Rana
C. Dr. J.C. Arya D. Dr. C.L. Mohan

164. Who was Manipur's first lady medical Doctor?
A. Manorama Devi
B. Thangjam Ongbi Bedamani Devi
C. N. Chidambara
D. Payal Ghosh

165. When was the first Operation Theatre opened in Manipur?
A. 1920 B. 1926
C. 1930 D. 1935

166. When was the first Hospital ward opened in Manipur?
A. 1925 B. 1928
C. 1930 D. 1931

167. Who was first Mr. Manipur?
A. P. Jugol B. Irom Leikhendra
C. R. Shyam D. Ranabir Meitei

168. Who is the Manipur's first Mr. India?
A. M. Gopal Sharma B. K. Dilip Singh
C. Nongthongbam Maipak D. M. Phanjoubam

169. Who is the author of the book ''Manipur: The Jewel of India''?
A. E. Ishwarjit Singh B. S.C. Joshi
C. L.R. Singh D. H. Guno Singh

170. Who is the author of the book ''Madhabi''?
A. Kh. Chaoba B. R.K. Shitaljit
C. Dr. Komal Singh D. Lal Dena

---

161. A **162.** C **163.** A **164.** B **165.** B **166.** D **167.** B **168.** C **169.** B **170.** C

171. Who is the author of the book 'Mao : The Naga Tribe of Manipur?

A. Lorho Mary Maheo | B. Naorem Sanajaoba
C. R. Constantine | D. H. Bhuban Singh

172. Where is Nupee Lal Memorial Complex located in Manipur?

A. Imphal | B. Moirang
C. Churachandpur | D. Moreh

173. Ruins of Citadel was built during the reign of :

A. King Jai Singh | B. King Khagemba
C. King Marjit | D. King Chourjit

174. Ruins of Citadel was built in the year :

A. 1500 A.D. | B. 1550 A.D.
C. 1600 A.D. | D. 1611 A.D.

175. Where is Shree Shree Govindajee Temple located?

A. Bishnupur | B. Kongla Fort
C. Old Langthabal Palace | D. Ukhrul

176. Who is the first Manipuri Child to get the Best Child Actor Award?

A. Leikhendra Singh | B. Ranbir Goswami
C. Shyam Singha | D. K. Narsingha

177. A veteran freedom fighter and a great socio-religious leader, Rani Gaidenliu was a living goddess for the manipuri people. Name the great Prime Minister of India who described her as "the daughter of the hills and gave the title "Rani of her people".

A. Lal Bahadur Shastri | B. Pandit Jawaharlal Nehru
C. Smt. Indira Gandhi | D. Morarji Desai

178. Which is the first Manipuri magazine started in 1917-18?

A. Longtai | B. Wakhal
C. Meitei Leima | D. Athouba

179. Which was the first Manipuri book to be awarded with the Telem Ningol Atoibema Award in children's literature?

A. Sana Kakchao | B. Ithak Ipom
C. Jahira | D. Ima

180. Who is the first Manipuri to win the Sangeet Natak Akademi Award?

A. H. Atomba Singh | B. T. Amudon Sharma
C. Bipin Singh | D. M. Amubi Singh

---

171. A **172.** A **173.** B **174.** D **175.** B **176.** A **177.** B **178.** C **179.** A **180.** D

181. Who is the first Manipuri to win a Gold Medal in Asian Games?
A. Ng. Dingko Singh B. Sanamacha Chanu
C. N. Kunjarani Devi D. M.C. Merrycom

182. Who is the first Manipuri to become a Union Minister?
A. Ng. Tompok Singh B. R.K. Jaichandra
C. R.K. Dorendra Singh D. N. Gouzagin

183. Who is the first Manipuri Film Actor?
A. Leikhendra Singh B. Robindro Sharma
C. Aribam Shyam Sharma D. M.A. Singh

184. Who is the first Manipuri Film Actress?
A. Gita Devi B. Manorama Devi
C. Rashi Devi D. Rashmi Devi

185. Who is the first Manipuri to win Rajiv Gandhi Khel Ratna Award?
A. Ng. Dingko Singh B. Thaiba Singh
C. M.C. MaryKom D. N. Kunjarani Devi

186. Who is the first Muslim Chief Minister of Manipur?
A. Md. Alimuddin Lilong Turel Ahanbi
B. Md. Abdul Qayum
C. Md. Ali Akbar
D. Javed Ahmed

187. Who is the first Manipuri Muslim Woman Advocate?
A. Noor Bano B. Benazir Majumdar
C. Fatima Shaikh D. Sabnam Noorani

188. What is the percentage of Muslim population as per 2011 census?
A. 22.40 B. 25.50 C. 8.40 D. 15.60

189. What is the area covered by the Manipuri Hockey field?
A. 200×20 Yards B. 200×40 Yards
C. 200×60 Yards D. 200×80 Yards

190. The historic 'International Polo Tournament' was held in Manipur in the year :
A. 1985 B. 1987
C. 1989 D. 1990

---

181. A **182.** B **183.** B **184.** C **185.** D **186.** A **187.** B **188.** C **189.** D **190.** D

191. In which year Oak Tassar was introduced in Manipur?
A. 1973-74 B. 1975-86
C. 1977-78 D. 1980-81

192. Who built the famous Vishnu temple situated at Bishenpur?
A. King Kyamba B. King Telheiba
C. King Tonaba D. King Punsiba

193. Sirohi National Park of Manipur got its recognition by the government in the year :
A. 1990 B. 1998
C. 1999 D. 2000

194. In which year was Yaingangpokpi Lakchao Wildlife Sanctuary opened :
A. 1989 B. 1991
C. 1995 D. 1998

195. The Manipur State Museum was inaugurated by which Prime Minister of India?
A. J.L. Nehru B. Indira Gandhi
C. Rajiv Gandhi D. A.B. Vajpayee

196. In which year Manipur University was upgraded as a Central University?
A. 1990 B. 1992
C. 1994 D. 1998

197. Which is the largest and most important mineral resource of Manipur?
A. Chromite B. Coal
C. Lignite D. Limestone

198. What is the hydro-electricity potential of Manipur?
A. 1784 MW B. 1700 MW
C. 1680 MW D. 1480 MW

199. In which year the first Manipur Panchayati Raj Bill was passed?
A. 1972 B. 1975
C. 1978 D. 1980

200. In which year Manipur got its own High Court?
A. 2010 B. 2011
C. 2013 D. 2012

---

191. A **192.** A **193.** B **194.** A **195.** B **196.** C **197.** D **198.** A **199.** B **200.** C

201. In which year the Indian Penal Code was first enacted in Manipur?
A. 1901 B. 1902
C. 1903 D. 1904

202. The number of Autonomous Hill District Councils in Manipur is :
A. 6 B. 9
C. 10 D. 12

203. The area covered by the Jiribam Rubber Farm is :
A. 800 hectares B. 889 hectares
C. 900 hectares D. 1050 hectares

204. Who was the Manipuri Muslim, popularly known as Japan Pitru?
A. Ali Akbar B. Alauddin Khan
C. Naqi Ahmed Choudhary D. Mehtab Ali

205. Which river flows from Manipur to Assam?
A. Barrak B. Thoubal
C. Iril D. Makru

206. Which is the largest grown agricultural product of Manipur?
A. Wheat B. Maize
C. Rice D. Orange

207. When was the old Cachar road constructed in Manipur?
A. 1530 B. 1532
C. 1534 D. 1536

208. Who constructed the old Cachar road?
A. Meidingu-Kabomba
B. James Johnstone
C. Yengkham Deksan Singh
D. J. K. Rajan

209. In which district was Khagemba's old palace situated?
A. Senapati B. Churachandpur
C. Tamenglong D. Ukhrul

210. Who was the first chief commissioner of Manipur?
A. Major General Rawal Amar Singh
B. Himat Singh
C. E. P. Moon Jan.
D. P. C. Mathew

---

201. D **202.** A **203.** B **204.** C **205.** A **206.** C **207.** D **208.** A **209.** B **210.** A

211. Who was the first Lieutenant Governor of Manipur?
A. D. R. Kohli
B. Baleswar Prasad
C. J. M. Raina
D. E. P. Moom

212. Loktak Lake is located in which district?
A. Bishnupur
B. Thoubal
C. Ukhrul
D. Tamenglong

213. Kachouphung Lake is located in which district?
A. Ukhrul
B. Bishnupur
C. Thoubal
D. Tamenglong

214. Barak waterfalls are located in which district?
A. Tamenglong
B. Bishnupur
C. Ukhrul
D. Senapati

215. Sangboo cave is located in :
A. Chandel
B. Ukhrul
C. Churachandpur
D. Imphal East

216. Height of Leikat Peak is :
A. 2,832 m.
B. 2,760 m.
C. 2,560 m.
D. 2,960m.

217. As per the 2011 census, the urban population of Manipur is :
A. 8, 34, 154
B. 9, 50, 325
C. 7, 90, 660
D. 10, 10, 548

218. As per the 2011 census, the rural population of Manipur is :
A. 20, 18, 224
B. 16, 20, 360
C. 20, 21, 640
D. 17, 10, 660

219. The State Emblem of Manipur is :
A. Singda Dam
B. Kangla Shaa
C. Shree Govindajee Temple
D. Khang Khui Cave

220. Kamjong district came into existance in :
A. 2016
B. 2015
C. 2014
D. 2013

---

211. B **212.** A **213.** A **214.** A **215.** A **216.** A **217.** A **218.** C **219.** B **220.** A

221. Which is the new district in Manipur?
A. Mao
B. Jiribam
C. Tamei
D. Moreh

222. As per the 2011 census which is the highly populated district in Manipur?
A. Thoubal
B. Bishnupur
C. Imphal West
D. Senapati

223. As per the 2011 census which is the less populated district in Manipur?
A. Ukhrul
B. Churachandpur
C. Chandel
D. Tamenglong

224. As per the 2011 census which is the most densely populated district in Manipur?
A. Imphal West
B. Thoubal
C. Bishnupur
D. Imphal East

225. As per the 2011 census which is the less densely populated district in Manipur?
A. Ukhrul
B. Tamenglong
C. Chandel
D. Churachandpur

226. What is the decadal growth rate (2001-11) of Manipur as per the 2011 census?
A. 20.01%
B. 25.02%
C. 24.50%
D. 32.03%

227. Which is the largest city in Manipur?
A. Kakching
B. Thoubal
C. Lilong
D. Imphal

228. Who is known as the "Lion of Manipur"?
A. Bir Tikendrajit
B. Hijam Irabat
C. Paona Brajabashi
D. Zilla Singh

229. Who is known as 'Mahakavi' in Manipur?
A. H. Guno Singh
B. Hijam Anganghal
C. Kh. Chaoba
D. Dr. Komal Singh

230. What is the hottest month in the State of Manipur?
A. July
B. August
C. September
D. June

---

221. B **222.** C **223.** D **224.** A **225.** B **226.** C **227.** D **228.** A **229.** B **230.** C

231. Where is the headquarters of Imphal East district?

A. Porompat B. Kirao Bitra
C. Sawombung D. Jiribam

232. Where is the headquarters of Imphal west district?

A. Lamsang B. Lamphelpat
C. Patsai D. Wangai

233. How many Tribes are recognised by the Government of Manipur?

A. 30 B. 31
C. 32 D. 35

234. Manipur 'Statehood Day' is celebrated on :

A. 25th February B. 13th August
C. 28th September D. 21st January

235. 'Manipuri Language Day' is celebrated on :

A. 20th August B. 28th September
C. 30th September D. 12th September

236. 'Manipur Integrity Day' is celebrated on :

A. 25th September B. 28th September
C. 23rd April D. 25th February

237. When was the State Institute of Journalism established?

A. 15th May 1990
B. 16th June 1994
C. 19th October 1992
D. 20th July 1995

238. When was the Council of Higher Secondary Education, Manipur established?

A. 1990 B. 1991
C. 1992 D. 1993

239. Manipur Human Rights Commission, Lamphelpat was established on :

A. 20th June 1995
B. 27th June 1998
C. 11th May 1990
D. 15th June 1992

240. Bunning wildlife sanctuary is situated in which district?

A. Imphal East B. Tamenglong
C. Chandel D. Churachandpur

---

231. A **232.** B **233.** C **234.** D **235.** A **236.** B **237.** C **238.** C **239.** B **240.** B

241. Which wildlife sanctuary has the largest area in Manipur?
A. Yaingoupokpi Lokchao B. Keilam
C. Zeliad D. Jiri Makru

242. Zeliad wildlife sanctuary is located in which district?
A. Chandel B. Tamenglong
C. Bishnupur D. Churachandpur

243. Which was the first English Journal of Manipur?
A. Meitei Leirang B. Manipur Mail
C. Sangai Express D. Manipur News

244. Who is the first Manipuri Film Producer?
A. Debkumar Bose
B. Karam Manmohan Singh
C. Kh. Pramodini
D. Aribam Shyam Sharma

245. Which was the first Manipuri Film to receive the President's Medal in the 20th National Film Festival?
A. Matamgi Manipur B. Langlen Thadoi
C. Imagee Ningthem D. None of these

246. First Arjuna and Rajiv Gandhi Khel Ratna Award winner for Manipur N. Kunjarani Devi is famous in which sport?
A. Cricket B. Hockey
C. Weightlifting D. Boxing

247. Suraj Lata Devi is related with which sport?
A. Hockey B. Weightlifting
C. Boxing D. Cricket

248. N. Dingko Singh is related with which sport?
A. Cricket B. Football
C. Hockey D. Boxing

249. Anita Chanu has fame in which sport?
A. Mountaineering B. Football
C. Tennis D. Cricket

250. The first National Games were held in Manipur in :
A. 1995 B. 1996
C. 1997 D. 1999

---

241. D **242.** B **243.** A **244.** B **245.** A **246.** C **247.** A **248.** D **249.** A **250.** D

251. Who was the editor of the "Manipur Paojel" in 1939?
A. Keisham Kunjabihari Singh   B. George Gordon
C. Dr. Brown   D. Hijam Irabat

252. Of the whole India, how much area is covered by Manipur State?
A. $\frac{1}{132}$ B. $\frac{1}{147}$
C. $\frac{1}{180}$ D. $\frac{1}{165}$

253. When was the "Clapped song" sung first time in Manipur?
A. 1830   B. 1847
C. 1857   D. 1870

254. Which jail in Manipur houses drug exclusively?
A. Shajiwa Jail   B. Imphal Jail
C. Jiribam Jail   D. None of these

255. When was the Manipur State Transport established?
A. 10th July, 1948   B. 15th August, 1949
C. 13th May, 1950   D. 20th April, 1952

256. When was the Manipur State Transport become a Corporation?
A. 20th July, 1972   B. 14th December, 1978
C. 27th March, 1976   D. 16th November, 1976

257. When does Manipur observe "Save Boundary Day"?
A. August 4, 1987   B. May 6, 1987
C. July 4, 1987   D. October 10, 1987

258. When did the King Gambhir Singh die?
A. 1831   B. 1832
C. 1833   D. 1834

259. When was the second "Nupi-Lal" (Women war against British) took place in Manipur?
A. 1939   B. 1940
C. 1941   D. 1942

260. Where is the Pony Breeding Project established in Manipur?
A. Tamenglong District   B. Senapati District
C. Bishnupur District   D. Chandel District

---

251. A **252.** B **253.** B **254.** A **255.** B **256.** C **257.** A **258.** D **259.** A **260.** B

261. When was the first Bank opened in Manipur State?
A. 1942 B. 1944
C. 1946 D. 1948

262. Manipur State Bank was opened in :
A. 1942 B. 1944
C. 1945 D. 1947

263. Who was the editor of the weekly jounral "Anouba Yug" in 1947?
A. Hijam Irabat Singh B. George Gordon
C. R.K. Bhubonsana D. Dr. Brown

264. During the reign of which king of Manipur the festival "Ningal Chackouba" was introduced?
A. Maharaja Tangjama
B. Maharaja Chandra-Kirti
C. Maharaja Garibnivaj
D. Maharaja Maramba

265. Who built the famous Lord Krishna temple situated in Imphal?
A. Nara Singha B. King Surchandra
C. King Charairongba D. King Kulachandra

266. When was the famous Lord Sanamahi temple built?
A. 1880 A.D. B. 1885 A.D.
C. 1890 A.D. D. 1891 A.D.

267. In which early part of the century Christianity came to Manipur?
A. 17th century B. 18th century
C. 19th century D. 20th century

268. Which song of Manipur is sung by only women?
A. Nat Ishei B. Nupi Pala
C. Ougri D. Pena Ishei

269. The creator of the Manipuri classical dance 'Ras Leela' was :
A. King Bhagyachandra Singh
B. King Chingthang Khomba
C. King Ningthou Khomba
D. King Madhuchandra

270. Nongthombam Maipak got the 'Mr. India' title in the year :
A. 1967 B. 1968
C. 1969 D. 1970

---

261. C **262.** D **263.** A **264.** B **265.** C **266.** D **267.** D **268.** B **269.** A **270.** D

271. In which year Sougaijam Somorendra Singh became the first graduate from Manipur?
A. 1920 B. 1925
C. 1932 D. 1935

272. The Aimol, Purum, Kom, Koireng and Chiru are the sub-tribes of which tribe?
A. Konrem B. Mao
C. Angami D. Kacha Naga

273. Manipur Agro-Industries Coporation was set-up in :
A. 1992 B. 1993
C. 1994 D. 1995

274. What is the total area under cultivation of different crops in Manipur?
A. 2, 50, 000 hectares B. 2, 60, 000 hectares
C. 2, 85, 000 hectares D. 3, 00, 000 hectares

275. Which district is the largest producer of Sugarcane in Manipur?
A. Chandel B. Imphal west
C. Bishnupur D. Thoubal

276. Yangmaso Shaiza was the first tribal :
A. Chief Minister of Manipur
B. Chief Commissioner of Manipur
C. M.P. from Manipur
D. Governor of Manipur

277. How many seats are reserved for scheduled castes in Manipur?
A. 1 B. 2
C. 3 D. 4

278. "Manipur Municipality Act" was introduced in the urban areas of the state in the year :
A. 1971 B. 1973
C. 1976 D. 1978

279. The total area covered by the Manipur Valley is :
A. 1800 sq. kms. B. 1843 sq. kms.
C. 1860 sq. kms. D. 1875 sq. kms.

280. What is the height of Mount Tenipu?
A. 2910 metres B. 2950 metres
C. 2970 metres D. 2994 metres

---

271. A **272.** A **273.** A **274.** C **275.** D **276.** A **277.** A **278.** C **279.** B **280.** D

281. With which country Manipur shares an international border?
A. Myanmar B. China
C. Bangladesh D. None of these

282. Mount Tenipu is located in which district of Manipur?
A. Tamenglong B. Senapati
C. Thoubal D. Bishnupur

283. Jananeta Irabat's birthday is celebrated on :
A. 20th October B. 30th November
C. 30th September D. 18th September

284. The biggest source of the state income of Manipur is :
A. Industry B. Forest Resource
C. Agriculture D. None of these

285. The State Anthem of Manipur was composed by :
A. B. Jayanta Kumar B. K. Kunjabihari
C. A. Thambou Singh D. Sagolsem Indramani

286. L.M.S. Law college stands for :
A. Lairenmayum Seibyasachi Law College
B. Lairenmayum Sobita Law College
C. Longjam Mani Singh Law College
D. Liberal Manipur Society Law College

287. Manipur's first eastern dam Khoupum Dam is situated on which river?
A. Imphal river B. Manchandui river
C. Iril river D. Nambul river

288. In which district Khoupum Dam is located?
A. Bishnupur B. Thoubal
C. Ukhrul D. Tamenglong

289. In which year was the Loktak Hydel Project commissioned?
A. 1980 B. 1981
C. 1982 D. 1983

290. Manipur's premier college Dhana Manjuri College (D.M. College) was established in the year :
A. 1946 B. 1947
C. 1948 D. 1949

---

281. A **282.** B **283.** C **284.** C **285.** A **286.** A **287.** B **288.** D **289.** D **290.** A

291. In which part of Manipur bamboo forests are abundantly grown?

A. Eastern Part
B. South western Part
C. South Northern Part
D. Northern Part

292. Who is the author of the Jamini Gold Medal award winner novel "Khudol"?

A. Pacha Meitei
B. E. Nilakanta Singh
C. Hijam Guno Singh
D. A. Chitreshwar Sharma

293. Who was the author of the 18th century book called "Sana Manik"?

A. E. Sonamani Singh
B. R.K. Madhubir
C. Wahengbam Madharam
D. Sudhir Naoraibam

294. Who wrote "Elisa Amagi Mahao"?

A. Nilabir Sharma Shastri
B. Arambam Biren Singh
C. G.C. Tongbra
D. N. Kunjamohan

295. Padmashree Award winner author who translated 'Mahabharata' book in Manipuri is :

A. Ch. Kalachand Shastri
B. Birendrajit Naorem
C. Ningombam Sunita
D. N. Ibobi Singh

296. Luira is a festival of which tribe?

A. Thadou
B. Tangkhul
C. Kabui
D. Kuki

297. Which popular form of festival is observed by Kuki tribes?

A. Chumpha
B. Chavang Kut
C. Gan Ngai
D. None of these

298. Who was Manipur's first to get Lalit Kala Akademi Award?

A. T.A. Mudon Sharma
B. T. Kunja Kishore Singh
C. Th. Tombi Singh
D. Y. Gambhini Devi

299. In the reign of which king 'Heigru Hitongba' was started in Manipur?

A. King Irengba
B. King Chandra Kirti
C. King Surchand Singh
D. King Meidingu Loitongba

300. The game of 'Kong' flourished during the reign of :

A. King Ningthou Kongba
B. King Laitongba
C. King Keiphaba
D. King Khomba

---

291. B **292.** C **293.** C **294.** D **295.** A **296.** B **297.** B **298.** C **299.** A **300.** B

301. How many gold Medals were won by Manipur in the Vth National Games?
A. 40 B. 45
C. 49 D. 55

302. R. K. Singhajit got Padmashree for his work in :
A. Dance B. Literature
C. Drama D. Education

303. As per the 2011 census which district have the highest literacy rate?
A. Imphal East B. Imphal west
C. Bishnupur D. Churachandpur

304. When was Manipur Human Rights Commission established?
A. 25th May 1995 B. 27th June 1999
C. 27th June 1998 D. 28th April 1996

305. As per the 2011 census what is the Males population of Manipur?
A. 1,438,586 B. 1,105,680
C. 1,516,123 D. 1,315,219

306. As per the 2011 census what is the Females population of Manipur?
A. 1,170,338 B. 1,417,208
C. 1,330,216 D. 1,175,670

307. The Kabaw Valley was handed over to Myanmar (Burma) in the year :
A. 1830 B. 1834
C. 1838 D. 1840

308. When was the first English school established in Manipur?
A. 1880 B. 1885
C. 1890 D. 1892

309. Why was Manipur Durbar established in 1907?
A. To assist the British in the administration of Manipur
B. To assist the Government of India in the administration of Manipur
C. To assist the Maharaja in the administration of Manipur
D. None of these

310. The Manipuri Kings who got title of KCSI (Knight Commander Service of India) are :
A. Chandrakriti and Churachand Maharaja
B. Surchandra and Churachand Maharaja
C. Budhachandra and Surchandra Maharaja
D. Chandrakriti and Budhachandra Maharaja

---

301. C **302.** A **303.** B **304.** C **305.** A **306.** B **307.** B **308.** B **309.** C **310.** A

311. What is the full form of MOA?
- A. Manipur Olympic Association
- B. Manipur Oil Association
- C. Manipur Organisation of Adults
- D. None of these

312. In which year was 'Manipur women's Football Association' formed?
- A. 1972
- B. 1976
- C. 1980
- D. 1982

313. Who was the 'founder patron' of modern sports movement in Manipur?
- A. Charairongba
- B. Keiphaba Yanglon
- C. Sir Churachand Singh
- D. Bhadra Singh

314. Who is the author of the book 'My Experience in Manipur'?
- A. Sir James Johnstone
- B. Lucy Zehol
- C. A.K. Paul
- D. E.W. Dun

315. In Manipur 'Durga Puja' is locally known as:
- A. Heikru Hitongba
- B. Kwak Yatra
- C. Yaoshang
- D. None of the above

316. What is the height of Saheed Minar?
- A. 45 feet
- B. 50 feet
- C. 55 feet
- D. 60 feet

317. L. Nabakishore Singh got Padamshree for his work in :
- A. Theatre
- B. Literature
- C. Dance
- D. Herbal Medicine

318. Ksh. Thouranisabi Devi got Padamshree for her work in :
- A. Nat Songkritan
- B. Mountaineering
- C. Cinema
- D. Boxing

319. Where is Sainik School situated in Manipur?
- A. Imphal
- B. Bishnupur
- C. Senapati
- D. Ukhrul

320. Who is known as the 'Melody King' in Manipur?
- A. R.K. Bhogen
- B. Nongmaithem Pahari
- C. S. Devabrata Singh
- D. L. Lakpati Singh

---

311. A **312.** B **313.** C **314.** A **315.** B **316.** C **317.** D **318.** A **319.** A **320.** B

321. Who is known as the 'Melody Queen' in Manipur?
A. Sabitri Heisnam B. Y. Gambhini Devi
C. Laishram Mema Devi D. Y. Ranjana Devi

322. Who is popularly known as the 'Jananeta' (leader of the people) in Manipur?
A. L. Jugeswar Singh B. N. Tombi Singh
C. Paokai Hao Kip D. Hijam Irabat

323. Which is the biggest Temple in Manipur?
A. Shree Shree Govindajee Temple
B. Vishnu Temple
C. Hanuman Thakur Temple
D. Radha Raman Temple

324. Which is the biggest cave in Manipur?
A. Khu Kse B. Khang Khui Cave
C. Sangboo D. Tonglon

325. How many tribal dialects are recognised by the government of India in Manipur?
A. 2 B. 4
C. 5 D. 6

326. Which is the highest rainfall area in Manipur?
A. Thoubal B. Ukhrul
C. Tamenglong D. Chandel

327. Which is the lowest rainfall area in Manipur?
A. Senapati B. Imphal
C. Ukhrul D. Churachandpur

328. Where is Orange Festival celebrated in Manipur?
A. Tamenglong B. Ukhrul
C. Senapati D. Bishnupur

329. The present 10+2+3 system of education was started in Manipur from the academic session of :
A. 1985-86 B. 1986-87
C. 1988-89 D. 1990-91

330. What is Jhum cultivation locally called in Manipur?
A. Mono B. Kamlou
C. Pamlou D. Tuwalu

---

321. C **322.** D **323.** A **324.** B **325.** D **326.** C **327.** D **328.** A **329.** B **330.** C

331. How many small Town committees are in Manipur?
A. 20
B. 25
C. 33
D. 35

332. How many number of Municipalities are in the Urban areas of Manipur?
A. 9
B. 12
C. 16
D. 18

333. "INAMPEILIN' is the annual festival of which tribe of Manipur?
A. Maring
B. Tongkhul
C. Chothe
D. Tarao

334. What does 'MASLSA' stand for?
A. Manipur State Legal Services Authority
B. Manipur State Legal Society Authority
C. Manipur Strong Legal Society Association
D. None of these

335. When was the status of chief commissioner upgraded to Lieutenant Governor in Manipur?
A. 1968
B. 1969
C. 1970
D. 1971

336. Who is the first Manipuri Women Film Producer?
A. Sabitri Heisnam
B. Y. Ranajana Devi
C. Khaidem Sakhi Devi
D. K. O. Thouranisabi Devi

337. Manipur State Gazette was first launched in the year :
A. 1929
B. 1930
C. 1931
D. 1932

338. Who was the first Teacher (Manipuri) to have taught in School?
A. Mayanglambam Purna Singh (1893)
B. Ch. Kalachand Shastri (1860)
C. R.K. Jhalajit Singh (1870)
D. G. Surchand Sharma (1880)

339. Who was the first Director of Education in Manipur?
A. M.S. Sharma (1960-61)
B. S.D. Bahuguna (1958-59)
C. C. Kirti Singh (1972-73)
D. K.C. Tongbra (1975-76)

340. Which lake is known as the "Kohinoor of Manipur"?
A. Zailad Lake
B. Kachouphung Lake
C. Loktak Lake
D. Kharung Lake

---

331. C **332.** A **333.** C **334.** A **335.** B **336.** C **337.** D **338.** A **339.** B **340.** C

341. What is the oldest salt mine (brine) in Manipur?
A. Ningel salt mine
B. Sikhong salt mine
C. Chandrakhong salt mine
D. Waikhong salt mine

342. Where is rubber grown in Manipur?
A. Kakching B. Jiribam
C. Nambal D. Machi

343. When does the "Manipur Plantation Crops" establish?
A. 1985-86 B. 1990-91
C. 1979-80 D. 1981-82

344. Where is the hottest place in Manipur?
A. Tengnoupal B. Moirang
C. Jiribam D. Kakching

345. Who was the first person to set up NCC in Manipur?
A. L.H. Harnet B. H. Tombi Singh
C. P.K. Suisy D. P. K. Behring

346. Who is the first Manipuri Chief Justice ?
A. P. Jugal B. R. K. Manisama Singh
C. Ranbir Meitei D. K. Sanatomba

347. The district of Manipur which is known as the birth place of Christianity in the state is :
A. Thoubal B. Senapati
C. Ukhrul D. Chandel

348. The Number of tea gardens in Manipur is :
A. 4 B. 6
C. 10 D. 12

349. In which year Oak Tassar Project was introduced in Manipur?
A. 1971-72 B. 1975-76
C. 1973-74 D. 1978-79

350. Bir Tikendrajit Singh's crusade was against the :
A. Chinese B. Japanese
C. Burmese D. Britishers

---

341. A **342.** B **343.** D **344.** C **345.** A **346.** B **347.** C **348.** B **349.** C **350.** D

351. Takhel Khong (Tripura Canal) was Constructed by :
A. Khabomba B. Punsiba
C. Telheiba D. Bharatsai

352. Manipur state Durbar was established in :
A. 1905 B. 1906
C. 1907 D. 1908

353. In which district Nungba Sub-division is located?
A. Thoubal B. Jiribam
C. Noney D. Ukhrul

354. How many Nagar Panchayats are in Manipur?
A. 15 B. 16
C. 17 D. 18

355. When was the war of Independecne or the Anglo-Manipur war held?
A. 1890 B. 1891
C. 1895 D. 1897

356. When did the Chandel district come into existence?
A. May 13, 1974 B. July 6, 1977
C. June 10, 1978 D. Septerber 5, 1980

357. When was the 'Fast Tract Court' established in Manipur?
A. October 5, 2001 B. November 6, 2002
C. January 7, 2003 D. July 5, 2001

358. When did Manipur Sales Tax Act & Rules come into force?
A. December 10, 1990 B. June 5, 1980
C. May 20, 1985 D. August 6, 1995

359. Manipur Public Service Commission was formed in :
A. 1972 B. 1973
C. 1974 D. 1975

360. Who was the first chairman of the Manipur Public Service Commission?
A. S. K. Behring
B. G. B. K. Hooja
C. K. L. Sharma
D. P. Krishnamohan Singh

---

351. A **352.** C **353.** C **354.** D **355.** B **356.** A **357.** A **358.** A **359.** A **360.** B

361. Who was the first secretary of the Manipur Public Service Commission?
A. Ch. Abhijit Singh
B. Ph. Shyamananda Sharma
C. Karam Goura Kishore Singh
D. Ch. Dhanbir Meitei

362. When was the Manipur Science & Technology Council established?
A. 1980 B. 1985
C. 1988 D. 1990

363. What is the total area of Manipur under forest cover?
A. 16000 sq km. B. 16538 sq km.
C. 17346 sq km. D. 17503 sq km.

364. How many Gram Panchayats are there in Manipur?
A. 150 B. 155
C. 161 D. 165

365. Thanlon is located in which district?
A. Pherzawl B. Imphal West
C. Senapati D. Tamenglong

366. Phungyar is located in which district?
A. Bishnupur B. Thoubal
C. Kamjong D. Chandel

367. The book 'Fragments of Manipuri Culture' was written by :
A. E. Nilakanta Singh B. G. K. Ghosh
C. R. K. Shitaljit D. M. K. Binodini

368. The book 'Ima' was written by :
A. L. Premchand B. Hijam Angahal
C. Lucy Zehal D. E. W. Dun

369. The book 'Sur Vigyan' recognised by the state government as a text book for music in Manipur is written by :
A. H. Guno Singh B. E. Nilakanta Singh
C. Laishram Memma D. R. K. Madhubir

370. In Manipur who was popularly known as Bob?
A. Birendrajit Naorem B. Aribam Shyam Sharma
C. M. A. Singh D. Ralengnao Khaling

---

361. C **362.** B **363.** C **364.** D **365.** A **366.** C **367.** A **368.** D **369.** C **370.** D

371. Who is known as the 'Father of Manipuri Dance and Style'?
A. Guru Amubi Singh
B. Guru T. Amudon Sharma
C. Guru Bipin Singha
D. Guru L. Kaireng Singh

372. Who is honoured with the title 'Nritya Rani'?
A. L. Ibemhal Devi
B. Elam Indira Devi
C. H. Ngangbi Devi
D. Darshana Jhaveri

373. Who is the first recipient of the Manipuri children's literature award named 'Telam Ningal Atoibema Award'?
A. R. K. Bhubonsana
B. S. Surchand Sharma
C. M. Kirti Singh
D. M. K. Binodini Devi

374. Which place is called the 'Rice Basket of Manipur'?
A. Kumbi
B. Kwakta
C. Kakching
D. Samurou

375. The Meitei language has its own script. The name of script is :
A. Meitei Mayek
B. Devnagari
C. Sabrai
D. None of these

376. Which of the following highways did not pass through Manipur?
A. NH-39
B. NH-53
C. NH-150
D. NH-35

377. The total length of National Highways in Manipur is :
A. 850 kms.
B. 900 kms.
C. 1317 kms.
D. 1000 kms.

378. Who was the first General Secretary of the Manipuri Sahitya Parishad established in 1935?
A. Hijam Irabot
B. Gokulchandra Singh
C. Laitman Yaima
D. A. Thambou Singh

379. Sirohi National Park is located in which district of Manipur?
A. Imphal East
B. Chandel
C. Tamenglong
D. Bishnupur

380. Where is 'Khansari Sugar Factory' located in Manipur?
A. Khangabok
B. Iraishemba
C. Kabowakching
D. Kadamtala

---

371. C **372.** B **373.** A **374.** C **375.** A **376.** D **377.** C **378.** A **379.** A **380.** A

381. Where is 'Mechanised Dye House' located in Manipur?
A. Iroishemba B. Takyel
C. Loitang Khunou D. Kabowakching

382. Around which plant all Manipuri marriage ceremonies are conducted?
A. Sirai Lily B. Pineapple
C. Tulsi D. Orange

383. The Gostha Lila dance of Manipur is also known as :
A. Panshenba B. Manshenba
C. Sanshenba D. None of these

384. Which is the biggest festival celebrated by the Kabui Naga tribe of Manipur?
A. Gan Ngai B. Kut
C. Cheiraoba D. Chumpha

385. Manipuri folk dance 'Thabal Chongba' is associated with which festival?
A. Lai Haraoba B. Yaoshang
C. Rath Yatra D. Heikru

386. How many types of Kauna are available in Manipur?
A. Two B. Three C. Four D. Five

387. How many types of 'Yenpak' are used by the people of Manipur?
A. Four B. Six C. Three D. Seven

388. Who was the last Chairman of Manipur Territorial Council 1957?
A. M. Koireng Singh B. S. Meenakitan
C. Dr. P. Kamal D. Vimal Laishram

389. Who wrote 'Bor Saheb Ongbi Sanatombi' and 'Nungairakta Chandramukhi'?
A. E. Sonamani Singh B. M. K. Binodini
C. N. Ibobi Singh D. G. C. Tongbra

390. Which was Manipur's first book to be awarded Sahitya Academy (National) Award?
A. Imphal Amasugn Magi Ising— Nugsheetki Phibam
B. Aseibagi Nitaipog
C. Ngabongkhao
D. Kalenthagi Leipaklei

---

381. A **382.** C **383.** C **384.** A **385.** B **386.** A **387.** C **388.** A **389.** B **390.** A

391. "Naga Lui Ngaini" which is a festival of Naga people relates to :

A. New year
B. Seed sowing
C. Harvesting
D. None of these

392. "Phait Lam, Dak Lam, Silam Lam" are the dance forms of :

A. Mao Maram
B. Paite
C. Tangkhul
D. None of these

393. The 55 feet high Monument of Shaheed Minar was constructed by well-known sculptor :

A. M. Priyo Kumar
B. Mohit Paul
C. Ramesh Paul
D. Mahendra Mani Singh

394. Who among the following sportpersons is nominated in Rajya Sabha in 2016?

A. N. Kunjarani Devi
B. Suranjoy Singh
C. N. Dingko Singh
D. M.C. Mary Kom

395. What was the former name of the present Paona Bazar of Manipur?

A. Sardar Bazar
B. Maxwell Bazar
C. Prem Bazar
D. Ongbi Bazar

396. Manipur's biggest masjid 'Sardar Bazar Jama Masjid' was constructed in the year :

A. 1890
B. 1896
C. 1875
D. 1885

397. Who among the following sportpersons of Manipur got Rajiv Gandhi Khel Ratna Award in 2018?

A. L. Devendro Singh
B. Y. Penubala Chanu
C. O. Bembem Devi
D. Mirabai Chanu

398. Meitram Bir Award is given in the field of :

A. Manipuri Drama
B. Sport
C. Education
D. Social Service

399. The first treaty of Anglo Manipuri Alliance was signed in the year :

A. 1750
B. 1755
C. 1758
D. 1762

400. In which year the 'Treaty of Yandaboo' was made?

A. 1820
B. 1830
C. 1826
D. 1840

1910

---

391. B **392.** B **393.** C **394.** D **395.** A **396.** B **397.** D **398.** A **399.** D **400.** C

www.ingramcontent.com/pod-product-compliance
Lightning Source LLC
Chambersburg PA
CBHW071802090426
42737CB00012B/1918
* 9 7 8 9 3 5 0 1 2 7 0 3 2 *